I'm Still Trying To Figure It All Out Myself...

Larry Cohen's book is a delight! His vast experience working with children and his passion for life speak to the reader in an honest and no nonsense manner. Good sense and great advice make this a charming read for all ages.
–Helen Foerstel Cooke, B.A., Sociology/Anthropology, Former Student

[This] book. . .resonated with me. His stories about common sense wisdom told through the lens of everyday, ordinary life experiences are enlightening, inspiring and funny. Don't let the book's title mislead you. Larry has indeed figured it all out. His knowledge and wisdom will inspire you to lead a more positive and rewarding life. I think this book should be required reading for all students. Maybe someday it will.
–Lisa Gueli Regnante, Columnist for the Howard County Times, B.A., Communcations, Former Student

I couldn't put it down. This is one of those books you keep on a shelf and periodically pull it out when something is troubling you. This is certainly a book that makes one think about behavior, morals, values, and life, and it encompasses all aspects of humanity. I am certain that anyone who reads this book will view life with a bit more meaning, and hopefully will see how the various aspects interrelate and affect how fulfilling a person's life will ultimately become. As a parent of teenage boys, I would like nothing more than to have them sit and read this book.
–Karen Kaberle Wootton, Director of Admissions, Glenelg Country School, M.S., School Administration, Former Student

Sage advice with a tincture of common sense ... Larry Cohen delivers an inspirational account of raising children, traversing adolescence, relating to others, and the neverending experience of "making choices." At times inspirational and at others, downright funny! Larry captures the human condition with a profound sense of hope and honesty. Life is what you want it to be...and if it is not exactly

what you wanted....it can still be great. Take Larry's advice....stop the nonsense and love life!
–Eileen O'Brien, Ph.D., Psychology, Catholic University, Friend

This book invites you into an insightful, authentic and genuine conversation that will stimulate the reader's journey of personal reflection. It addresses life matters with both simplicity and depth. Larry Cohen's observations and advice exemplify why Father knows best!
–J. Gerald Suarez, Ph.D., Organizational Psychology, University of Puerto Rico, Friend

Common sense life lessons presented in an eloquent and enjoyably readable style... makes a great gift for anyone, but particularly for a young person embarking on life's journey.
–Al Tucci, Ph.D., UMCP, Human Resources and Education, Former Colleague, Friend

I'm Still Trying To Figure It All Out Myself...

by Larry Cohen

5/10

To [handwritten inscription] Thanks for your support. Enjoy. Larry Cohen

Ravenwater Press
Baltimore

Cover Design by Rus VanWestervelt
Cover Photo by Al Tucci

Published by Ravenwater Press, LLC
P.O. Box 20424
Baltimore, MD 21284
443.834.9489
www.ravenwater.com
ravenwaterpress@gmail.com

Printed by IndigoInk
9221 Rumsey Road, Suite S-6
Columbia, MD 21045
410.715.9071
www.indigoinkprint.com

Printed in the United States of America

Dedication

This book is dedicated to my family and friends, both living and deceased, who all helped shape my life. Included in this group are my wife and daughters, my parents, my siblings and their families, my in-laws, my extended family, my friends whom I grew up with, most of whom I am still fortunate enough to be friends with today, and all of the friends I've had since. (For the future, it is dedicated to any sons-in-law and grandchildren I might have.) It is also dedicated to my former teachers and coaches and the many teachers and administrators with whom I've worked through my years in education (thank you for what you have done for students) and to my former students everywhere (I hope you are all doing well and are living a happy, healthy, and successful life). It is also dedicated to all of the people who make a positive difference in the lives of other people on a daily basis and to everyone and anyone who wants to make a positive difference in this country and in this world. Everything you do matters. To each one it matters and makes a difference.

A very special thanks, always, to all of the people and individuals who do good things for society every day – our military personnel, police officers, firefighters, emergency workers, teachers and other educators, health professionals, social workers, and volunteers.

My intended audience is, first and foremost, my family, more specifically my wife and children. I want them to live a long, healthy, safe, and peaceful life filled with lots of love and happiness. This book is my message to them. I also intend this book for children everywhere and for teachers and parents and anyone else who cares about what happens in this world. I also wish you all health, happiness, peace and love. This book is my message to you as well. I encourage all of you to reflect on the thoughts and ideas discussed here and continue to commit yourselves to making a difference every day.

Special Dedication: In Memoriam

To my in-laws Abraham and Etta Unterberger. Abe was a survivor of the Holocaust and had the following number, A-18382, tattooed on his forearm at Auschwitz Concentration Camp, one of the many camps he passed through. He was very fortunate to have survived; millions were not.

This book is also dedicated to the memory of people I've known during my life who left us much too soon. Some were just children and never really even got started in life, some were in the middle and primes of their life, and some were just not with us long enough. *(If there is anyone I left out, I sincerely apologize. If you let me know, I will add their names to the website.)*

Diane Adams	Andrea Goldman	Betsy Parks
Janice Antonicelli	Michele Goldstein	Mike Parrish
Barry Aronson	Melissa Gorelik	Darin Pontell
Marty Askin	Candace Heisey	Brittany Phenicie
Andrea Barlow	Mark Hershkowitz	Alan Reid
Ellie Boussy	Marlene Horowitz	Esther Rosen
Jack Boussy	Rose Huber	Marvin Rosen
Allison Caldwell	Maura Hudson	Brittany Salmons
Walt Caldwell	Calvin Johnson	Chuck Sands
Scott Caplan	Kanika Johnson	Ann Scherr
Dennis Chandler	Mary Margaret	Al Schmall
Ronnie Chase	Kamerman	Jeffrey Schwartz
Paul Churchill	Heidi Kaplan	Peggy Secco
Terrence Costley	Ethel Kornbluth	Josh Siegert
Marianne Cross	Rabbi Samuel Landa	Casey Spence
Andrew Davis	Jon Loden	Katrina Tagget
Emily Davis	Linda Lurie	Ben Topus
Carol Doggett	Shara Lurie	Mark Tortora
Dan Dudek	Teddy Mann	Richie Vardaro
Patrick Epps	Jim McGregor	Ben Vassiliev
Norman Flecker	Ed Mitchell	Poinier Wadsworth
Larry Freer	Mike Morgan	Colleen Wall
Chet Gee	Steve Morris	Matt Watson
Bobby Globus	Jimmy O'Donnell	Valerie Whitely
Sandy Goldberg	Caprice Payne	Michael Wittenstein

GONE BUT NOT FORGOTTEN.
YOU WILL REMAIN IN OUR HEARTS FOREVER.

Table of Contents

W e all have different personalities. Our genetics, our environment, and our experiences help shape us. Some people say we are who we are. The question is: Can we change who we are and what we believe?

To a great extent, I think we can. But truly, only if we want to!

I am writing this as if I were talking to each one of you personally. I hope you will read it with this in mind.

I'm Still Trying To Figure It All Out Myself...does not mean that I'm trying to figure "it," being life itself, all out by myself, but that I'm trying to figure "it" (life) all out, "also" – like everyone else is trying to do.

Larry Cohen

Introduction

I have known Larry Cohen now, as I, Rachel, write this, for 28 years and 10 months – almost exactly to the day, when you take into consideration leap year, that is. And I, Susie, have known him for exactly 27 years. He is our father.

We are proud to have the opportunity to tell you a little bit about our Dad and the premise of his collection of thoughts and lessons contained within this work. I am calling it a work because it is artistic, humorous, thought provoking, story oriented and packed with educational lessons and moral insight. This work certainly defies the bounds of meeting criteria for living in a subdivided category like you might find when browsing around the bookstore or library. And I am calling it a thought-provoking piece that typifies who my father is and what he believes.

Though I am not perfect, a phrase you will hear frequently from my father too, I do my best every day and I attribute that quality to my parents. I could not have asked for two better people to raise me, nurture me, guide me, and support me through the trials, tribulations, and excitement of everyday life. Growing up, and continuing to today, my father has remained consistent in his actions and his values while leaving plenty of room for growth and new thought – a balance that many have yet to strike, if ever. It is not every individual who can, without doubt, behave in an ethical, moral, and supportive manner while straddling the ability to remain committed to his or her opinion, yet leave plenty of room for a change in mind or belief. These are the traits of a true parent, and true teacher, a true learner.

My dad possesses the emotional IQ of a genius! My sister and I can attest – we were provided with a sensitive ear whenever we needed one, and he always took the next step, a hard one – to provide the constructive feedback critical to our personal development. He and our mother built our confidence and consideration for the world and those around us on this foundation.

We were not the only ones. As you will read about in his work, our father is in frequent communication with the friends he grew up with, those he met as an adult, his colleagues from his work life, and a vast, vast number of students and their parents with whom he worked throughout his tenure in our public school system. We cannot go anywhere, even out of state, without our father running into someone that he knows, whose face lights up when they come into contact with him. He receives calls and emails from people all the time, looking for a chat or wanting to catch up, and especially looking for the advice of a wise mentor who can listen and help them work through a new or recurrent challenge. In some ways, our father is the "Dear Abby" of Howard County, Maryland (and even parts of his hometown NY).

We hope you enjoy the journey that our father Larry will take you on as you are reading this work. As we have continued to read through his thoughts and wisdom captured in the following pages, we are frequently reminded of the lessons and stories that he utilized as inputs for the playbook on raising good, healthy, and happy children and participating as a true and loving partner in marriage. Like any good playbook, you can review the chapters in any order you like or flip through to those that are the most consequential to you as you strategize about your present moment in time.

Come with your mind open and ready to absorb the insight, the humor and the experience of one absolutely great man, and remember that life is always an adventure; you never know what will come, but the people in your life, and the experiences that they have, provide an impressive and significant anthology of collective thought and knowledge. A substantial piece of our personal collections has been gifted to us by our father, Larry Cohen. We are convinced that you too will embrace these ideas and reflect upon them regularly as you face your own trials, tribulations, and adventures.

Enjoy.
Rachel L. Cohen
Susie Cohen

Foreword

I just turned 58 years old today, December 19, 2007, as I have just begun writing this book. I don't know how old I'll be when it's finished and how old I'll be when it's published. I hope sooner than later.

For your information: I am a retired educator from The Howard County Public School System in Howard County, Maryland. I've been a principal and teacher, among other positions in that school system. I am a native New Yorker, having grown up in Queens, New York. I am married to the same woman for 35 years now and we are the proud parents of two young adult daughters. I tell you all of this, just so you know my background. I readily admit that I am no smarter than anyone else here and like everyone else, I have my strengths and weaknesses. I'm just trying to make some points.

Why? Why am I writing this book? Simply put, it makes me feel that I'm doing something useful and productive. I believe it can help others, and I hope that at least some of what I say makes sense and helps make a difference in people's lives. I hope it inspires people to make this world a better place.

I often know some of the "who's, what's, when's, and where's" to life's many questions. It is the many "how's" and "why's" that I'd like the answers to. I'm still trying to figure that all out. If I ever do get the answers to the "why's" and "how's" in life, I'd like to think that I might just have it all figured out – and I really don't know that I or anyone else ever will. However, the pursuit of these answers is life itself. (If anyone ever claims to you that they have all the answers to this phenomenon we call life, be skeptical. They are, in my opinion, not being totally honest with you or themselves. They may have ideas, thoughts, and beliefs, yet I doubt very much that they have all of the answers. I haven't met that person yet.) However, I must admit that I'm still trying to figure it all out myself.

Here's what I think I understand and what I think I don't understand:

I understand our different personalities and the important impact of genetics in who we are, and the significant part that our environment and experiences also play in shaping us. I understand that there exists mental illness, emotional instability, different psychological problems and issues, and various physical and mental challenges. I understand the feelings of disappointment, frustration, and anger. I understand that all people are not equal in the sense of abilities and opportunities or in the sense of socio-economic standing. I know that all these conditions impact the behaviors of people. What I still don't understand is why these conditions exist in the first place. ("Life isn't fair" is the simple explanation.) What I also still don't understand, and refuse to accept, is prejudice, hate, hurting others, abuse, especially child abuse in any way, shape, or form, and basically the desire to hurt, harm, injure, and/or do anything to hurt yourself or others in any way. That stuff I don't get.

As we proceed through the book, I would like to share with you some of my thoughts and ideas. Right now I have more questions than I do answers. When you're done reading, there still may be more questions than answers, but at least I hope I've given you some ideas and thoughts to think about and some possible answers to some of the questions. Believe me, if I knew all of the answers, I'd be happy to tell you. Again, I'm still trying to figure it all out myself.

Preface

There are many wonderful people in the world who do many wonderful things. I even believe that most people do the right thing most of the time. However, two of my questions are: Why do humans sometimes act and behave as they do? Why do they interact with each other the way they do, at times negatively? I don't know the answer to these questions. I wish I did. That's part of what I'm still trying to figure out.

Life can be great. Life can be difficult. Life can be fun. Life can be challenging and stressful at times. Much of how life can be depends on us, our outlook on life in general, our attitude, our circumstances, and sometimes it even depends on the day. It depends on what we've done or not done, our attitude, our decisions and our choices, among other things. It also depends on other people's actions and behaviors. They do impact us, you know. That's a fact. How we react, however, is on us. We well know that we cannot control other people's behaviors and actions, but we can control our own behaviors and actions and our reactions and responses to other people's behaviors.

Most of the time I feel great. As I always say, "If I wake up, it's a good day." At those times, in particular, I think life is the greatest thing going. There are some times, I admit, though rather infrequently, when I'm not as happy and cheerful. In fact, I may even be sad – for one reason or another, or a combination of reasons. Why? It depends on circumstances. It may be something going on in my life in general at that time, something at work, something happening in the family, or something going on in the world that is bothering me. It may be a money issue or a health concern. I may feel overwhelmed or stressed. It can be something specific that is happening. It can be thinking about the past and missing my parents and/or other people who I was close to that were once a major part of my life. That can make me sad. After all, much of my life is already behind me. That's just a fact. It's not something I dwell upon; it just is what it is. (I would love to live forever – with my family and friends, of course. I know I can't do that.) So, it's usually something I can't do anything about at the time; it usually means that I can't control the outcome, as I would like to. When we lose control of a situation or we don't understand a situation or don't know what to do, or can't do anything about it, we may very well become frustrated, upset, and sad. Does that sound like any of you sometimes? To me, that's not unnatural. When we can't control something the way we would like to, frustration and sadness may set in. Is it the same way for all of us? I think it is. I know it is for me.

Of course, we all handle that frustration and sadness differently. For me, I tend to keep it in, pretty typical for a male (no sexist remark intended, that's just what the studies and research say – and I fit that mold), and I may become more sullen, short-tempered, and cranky. (I also am very much aware of the public behavior that I convey and the private, behind closed doors behavior. My public behavior does not change, or at least I don't believe it is noticeable. I may be more quiet than usual but the outside world would rarely, if ever, know. In cases where I am frustrated and sad, the private world and the private me does change. I am quieter, easier to anger, crankier, and probably more short-tempered. Again, I don't believe that is atypical. I don't justify it. It just is what it is. The inside world, the home, for most of us is typically the receiver of that frustration and sadness. Now the degree of that behavior, of course, depends on the individual. For me, it's just me being a pain to be around, basically not being as pleas-ant, humorous, and funny as I'd like to think I normally am. I'd like to think that I could control that better. That's not always the case.) However, I am very much aware of it and do try and control it bet-ter. It's usually short-lived as I always try and focus in on the many positives. That usually works for me. Being around other people and laughing also helps in these situations.

I admit that I am somewhat of a worrier. Actually I worry too much, probably much too much for any one person. I don't relax nearly as much as I should. I constantly worry about my family's health and safety. I know that. I've always been that way and I prob-ably always will. (Genetics? Environment? Experiences? I don't know.) I wish I didn't worry as much, and I know, logically, that worrying doesn't help things, change things, or make things any better. Yet I still do it. Though lately, I am getting a little better. I'm proud of myself for that, but it is still a battle. And despite the worrying, again, most of the time I'm pretty happy and upbeat. I always have been. I truly do enjoy living and life itself very much.

I look around at the world, this complex world as it is, and this great country of ours, the United States of America – the land of the free and home of the brave – and I say, why can't we all just get along? Why do we fight wars, struggle among ourselves, enslave and/or persecute people based on their race, religion, politics, ethnicity, gender, or sexual orientation? Why is that? Why do we, as human beings, allow that to happen? Why do some people hate others? Why do some people hurt others? Why are crimes and atrocities committed against fellow human beings? Can you imagine what we could accomplish if we all cooperated and worked together? Is that wishful thinking? I guess so. Is it naïve? Probably so. (Some people reading at this point might say, "This guy is so naïve – let him get real – this is the real world.") Okay, I can accept that; however, I encourage you to continue reading. And, you still haven't answered my question – Why? Please don't tell me it's just human nature. Is it human nature to kill, to persecute, to hate, to enslave? That's human nature? Who made that rule? That doesn't tell me anything. All that tells me is that we're willing to accept it as it is. Well, that's not acceptable to me; I'm not willing to just readily accept that excuse, or at least I'm going to question it and see if we can make it better, if even a little bit. You see, I admit, "I'm still trying to figure it all out myself." The operative word, admittedly, is "trying." We can't give up. We have to continue to try and make a difference.

Finally, I don't know why stuff happens. I wish I did know. I don't know why tragedy occurs in people's lives. I don't know why it happens to some and not others. I can't explain the cards that are dealt to any of us. I don't know why some people's lives are so hard and difficult and why some people have so much suffering and pain. I don't know why accidents occur that kill and injure people. I don't know why natural disasters happen that kill and harm people. I don't know why diseases occur that kill and cripple people. And, of course, I don't know why people, through their own actions, kill and hurt other people, either purposely or by "accident." I don't even know why or understand why people choose to hurt themselves. I wish I knew and I wish I had the power to stop all of those things and other bad things from happening. Again, quite honestly, "I'm still trying to figure it all out myself."

Having said all of that above, again, I hope this book will make a difference in people's lives and maybe together we won't solve it all, but we'll make some changes that will at least make it better for this person, for that person, for you, and for me. I have been very direct in some parts of the book, and it may make some people uncomfortable. If that's the case, I apologize. My purpose is certainly not to offend anyone but to make some poignant points. I may be even accused of being highly idealistic. That's okay. I'll take that criticism. Everything starts with ideals and visions. I believe strongly in what I say, and you can probably pick that up as you read. Some parts are heavy and some are lighter. I didn't know how to do it any other way.

I have begun each chapter with the title, "The Importance of...." I thought it was a good idea. We'll see. They are all important, in my view, and are not, by any means, in any particular order of priority. It's just how I arranged them as I began writing. Also, shorter or longer chapters do not mean that they are more or less important. It just turned out that way. Some I felt may have needed elaboration and others, not so much. I have incorporated some of the talks I have given to students and parents over the course of my career. They are pretty much verbatim with a couple of edits. There is some repetition and overlap because, first of all, overlap is almost impossible not to have and, second, I think repetition is important for ideas and thoughts to stick. These talks were given over a period of years so the repetition became both unavoidable and purposeful. For the students, I very much wanted the ideas and thoughts to stick and become part of their thought processes and habits. I also felt that it was important that they heard these messages as well as the adults.

I have tried to outline in the following chapters what I think is important to live a healthy, safe, successful, and happy life. Obviously there is no guarantee of that. I understand that. I don't like to accept that and that's certainly one of the reasons why I wrote this book. Again, I'm still trying to figure it all out myself. The reality is I don't know if I ever will. But, I'm still trying and we all need each other's help in doing it. This is not a "one person" process. It is an "everybody" process and destination. Hopefully you will all have some ideas and thoughts to share as well.

This is a work in progress and a working document for me that I hope to improve upon continuously. Life itself is a work in progress. Change does not come easy or happen overnight. For some of us this may mean big changes, and for some of us little changes, as the case may be. That's okay. We can do it. It is also a work in progress for all of us, and it is okay to ask for help and get advice and assistance from others. After all, we are an interdependent people – we depend on each other. That's okay. We need to do that.

I've tried to make this book perfect, but I'm not a perfectionist by nature. So, I did the best I could to make it the best I could. I just want it to be readable, and for it to make some sort of sense. It's me; it's who I am and it's what I believe. The main purpose of this book, again, is to help others and to give some tips and strategies that I think may help and may work to make this a better world. I'll keep trying and with all of your help and support, we'll make some changes. Maybe we won't find all of the answers to life's many questions, but hopefully we'll get closer and we'll all be better off for it.

Thank you for taking time to at least read the Introduction up to this point. I hope you will take time to read the rest of the book; more than that, I hope that you will sincerely follow up with your own thoughts and comments by e-mailing me. I also hope to add comments to my website on a regular basis.

As you try to figure it all out, remember, I'm also still trying to figure it all out myself.

Acknowledgments

I would like to thank the following people for reading the original manuscript and providing me with input and feedback. Thank you so much for your time and comments. I really appreciate it.

Charlie Ashcraft	Jen McKechnie
Nadine Bernard	Chris Myers
Matt Brumberger	Eileen O'Brien
Michael Cohen	Jen Peduzzi
Rachel Cohen	Sandy Queen
Rita Cohen	Lisa Regnante
Susie Cohen	Elaine Reid
Helen Cooke	Karl Schindler
Ivan Croft	Sally Schiomichi
Catherine Garris	Richard Schreibstein
Patricia Gordon	Amy Strahl
Beverly Hertz	Gerald Suarez
Alan Horowitz	Al Tucci
Addie Kaufman	Rus VanWestervelt
Karen Mason	Brenda VonRautenkrauz
Diane McCarthy	Lynn Voyton

Karen Wootton

I would like to thank the following people:

My friend Richard Schreibstein for his legal counsel in helping getting the book published.

My friend Chris Myers for his much appreciated guidance and support throughout the entire process.

My friend and publisher Rus VanWestervelt for his guidance, support, encouragement and assistance in getting this book published. Without you Rus, it may never have happened. Thank you for your hard work, your dedication and, most of all, your belief in the book and your belief in me.

Finally I would like to thank my wife, Rita, our girls Rachel and Susie, and all of my friends, colleagues and former students who encouraged me to write this book. I sincerely appreciate your confidence and support.

I'm Still Trying To Figure It All Out Myself...

*In loving memory of my parents,
Joseph and Jeanette Cohen.*

1

The Importance of
Family and Parenting

Home is home. A house is not necessarily a home. A home is made up of people, not things. I've been to many houses that are not homes. Some of them are museums – don't touch this, don't sit on that, takc off your shoes, watch where you walk, etc. I felt like it should be roped off.

I've been to other houses that are very comfortable and very welcoming. They are homes. Home is where we should feel most secure and safe. It is the place where we learn the most, and it is the place where we model what we see, what we hear, what we watch and what we observe. As parents – myself included, we have an awesome responsibility. In my view, our priorities need to revolve around our children. We need to make choices and decisions that are in the best interests of our children. Nothing is more important than our children's health, safety, and welfare – their physical health, their emotional health, their mental health, their physical safety, and their general welfare. That is, and should always be, our number one priority, and I don't care how old they are. I believe most, if not all parents, truly believe that. We are our children's allies and advocates – always and forever. We are their protectors. We are their caregivers. We are their "best friends" in the truest sense of the word because, again, we are their allies, their advocates, their supporters, and their guides. We give them encouragement, confidence, and a sense of security. We praise them when they do well, we discipline them with love, caring, and respect, and correct them when they are wrong. We teach them right from wrong. It's okay; in fact it's advisable to have consequences for misbehavior. It's not okay to abuse or otherwise injure, harm, or do damage to a child physically, verbally, emotionally, or otherwise. Children are to be protected and cared for at all times. The love we give should be consistent and unconditional. There are no strings attached to the love of our child. They are going to make mistakes. I know we made mistakes when we were young. We teach them and model for them so that those mistakes are kept to a minimum and do not impact their health and safety or the health and safety of others. We teach them to learn from their mistakes and not to repeat the same mistake twice.

In the home, we adults must also treat each other with love, trust, and respect. Our relationship as parents among ourselves, our children, and other adults will model for our children the behavior that we expect and value.

Children see everything we say and do. They will learn what to do more from our actions than our words.

As a family, we are also responsible for their education. Yes, of course the school plays a major role in that. However, we are their first and foremost teacher, and it is our involvement and our support that will help them be successful in school. School is a place of learning and education is a partnership - and we, as the parents, are one of those partners, if not the major one. Never underestimate our influence on how well our children do in school.

We have to support our children, and we have to work with

our schools to ensure that our children get a quality education. We need to emphasize education and make it important in our household. If we don't make it important it is going to be more difficult for our child to be successful in school and later in life. I have never met a parent yet who did not want the best for their child, though some may not have known the best way to go about it.

Our home should be caring and warm, safe and secure, a learning environment, a place where we and our children want to be and a place that is welcoming to them and others, especially to their friends. (If they're in our house, then we can keep a better eye on them.) People have got to feel comfortable there. Why some families do not get along, why they fight, and why there is abuse in some of them, quite honestly, is what I'm still trying to figure out myself.

FROM A SPEECH TO PARENTS:
ON FAMILY AND PARENTING

So we thought this job of parenting was going to be easy. So we thought raising a family would be a piece of cake. Welcome to the real world. I know we have no regrets, but we do have some challenges. Parenting is a full-time job. It is truly a 24 hours a day/7 days a week job. And it never ends. It is also a challenge to parent in a society that is constantly and continuously changing. Having said that, I do believe the basic tenets of good parenting still hold true. Please understand that our children have hopes and dreams as well as fears and concerns. We all do. They are no different. There is no parenting school, and often we either parent like our parents parented or we go in the opposite direction depending on how good or bad of a job we thought our own parents did. Sometimes, quite honestly, we are building the plane while flying it. I do urge all of us to please never parent out of anger, frustration, and/or rage. That does not serve anyone, especially our children, well. It is okay to be angry and frustrated, but it is not okay to act irrationally on that anger and frustration.

Understanding all of that, I think the best thing we can do as parents is be our children's allies and advocates, encourage them to follow their dreams and goals, teach them right from wrong, hold them responsible for their behaviors and actions, discipline them with love while having consequences for inappropriate behavior but never physically hitting or abusing our children, love them unconditionally, teach them respect, compassion, and empathy, give them encouragement, confidence, and a sense of security, show them how to be independent, yet understand that we will always be there to support them and listen to them, always keep the lines of communication open, be their guide, not their God, give them the confidence and encouragement to take good risks, maintain high but reasonable expectations for them, never expect perfection but expect their very best, model appropriate behavior ourselves, build a sense of consciousness and community within them, teach them how to laugh and have a good sense of humor, give them every opportunity and provide all of the necessary resources possible for them to be successful, teach them to be trustworthy, respectful, and responsible, and always make their health, safety, and happiness our number one priority.

The most important things we can give our children are our time, our unconditional love and affection, and our attention. Trust me, they will grow up very quickly and we never want to look back and be sorry for what we didn't do or did do. They will only be young for a very short while.

2
The Importance of Caring

To care or not to care – that's not the question. To me, it's not even an option. Of course we have to care. To care is to be concerned, to be interested, and to feel great affection and great love for somebody or some thing. To care is to feel that people are important, that something is important – so important that it requires our attention, our focus, our commitment, our concentration, our interest, and our love. How many times have I heard, "I don't care!"? I used to always tell students when they said that, "That's not true. The fact that you even said that indicates to me that you really do care." They'd smile. They knew they really cared.

Everyone cares about someone or something. The question is who and/or what do you care about and how much do you care? Caring is the first step in anything you do. Do you care about yourself? Do you care about your family? Do you care about your friends? Do you care about your job or career? Do you care about your health and safety? Everyone has to care about something. If we really don't care about any or all of those things we're headed for failure. **Rule #1**: You've got to care. **Rule #2**: Don't ever forget Rule #1. When we care we make decisions not just from our head and our brain, but from our heart, and that's okay.

When we care we generally put more thought into our decisions and choices, and we really think and ponder the options and choices we have. We also seriously consider the consequences of our decisions and choices when we care. When we don't care, anything goes and that's not okay. That's usually not in our best interest or anyone else's best interest. How would we like it if our doctor didn't care? Or if our pilot didn't care? Or if our financial advisor didn't care? As human beings we need to care about our family, our friends and our community, our country, our world, and ourselves. If we do care, we will do things to make things better for everyone.

I can't imagine anyone not caring at all about anything or anyone, including themselves. I am always baffled that, unfortunately, in my opinion, too many people care only about themselves and don't care enough or at all about others and the common good. Why not? We're all in this together.

From a speech to students:
On Caring

As human beings we must always remember to care about others, work to ensure that everybody is treated respectfully and fairly, and make sure that we genuinely care about other people, that we take pride in their successes as well as our own successes. And when we take joy in the successes of others, others will also gladly participate in our successes. We should all enjoy the successes of other people and only wish them the best. We need to be caring, we need to be nice, and we need to be kind. We need to work together to bring success to as many people as we can. "I care about you" is, in my opinion, the most important phrase and group of words there is. It's right up there with, "I love you." And if you don't think those words are important, just ask those people who think that they are not loved or cared about.

There's no question that people show their love and caring in different ways. With my own children and wife I say it. I say it with my mouth but it comes from my heart. Without fail, every telephone conversation, instant message or good-bye in person ends with, "Love you. Bye." It's part of who I am and who they are now. It just the way it is, and it's that way because we care. "I care" is more important than "I am" or "I know." To truly care one must think it and know it in their head and feel it and believe in their heart.

3
The Importance of
Education

Erasmus said, "The best hope of a nation lies in the proper education of its youth." How right he is. It is also said that education is the key to success. I think that's basically true and pretty accurate. Uneducated, or should I say undereducated people, have a more difficult time being successful. That's a given. It's not impossible to be undereducated and successful, but it is very difficult and challenging. However, how do we define educated and how do we define successful? I will try to define them to the best of my understanding.

Educated to me means having the ability to continue to learn, to be literate, to be able to think logically, and to process, explain, interpret, analyze, and synthesize information in some, but not necessarily all, areas. For example, I consider myself educated. I can do most of the above reasonably well in some areas – but not all areas. I can read and write, I understand history, and I understand some math; however, I don't understand science and computers very well. So, my point is, many of us are educated, but we have areas of strength and areas of weakness. I consider someone undereducated if they cannot perform any of these skills in any areas. (Notice that I'm continuing to use the word *undereducated* rather than *uneducated* because I would like to believe that everyone is educated in something.)

Defining success is a little bit more challenging. I guess I would define success as having attained, achieved, or accomplished the goals in life that one aspires to. I, of course, mean that in the most positive way. In other words, if someone hoped to be a teacher and achieved that goal, I would consider them successful. If someone aspired to be a plumber and achieved that goal, I would consider them successful. One dictionary defines success as the achievement of something planned or attempted. I like that definition.

Another definition the dictionary gives is "impressive achievement, especially the attainment of fame, wealth, or power." I don't particularly like the second part of that definition because I personally don't define success in terms of fame, wealth, or power. I much prefer the first definition. I believe that the role of education is to provide students the opportunity to be successful by giving them the knowledge, skills, experiences, and wisdom to continue to learn, to be lifelong learners, and to have the ability and potential to be successful in whatever path they choose to follow in life. My concern is that we are not successfully educating all of our children, even in this country, and that bothers me greatly.

Education is very important. It is critical for the survival of this country and the world in general. In my opinion, for any student in this nation not to be literate, to not know how to read, write, or do basic math is appalling and unacceptable. What an opportunity we are missing and what untapped human resources are out there that we are not reaching when we have children who are not literate. Part of it is that we are not all working together and we are not taking it seriously enough. Part of it is that the money that is needed is not as readily available as it should be, and part of it is that we have a lack of what I spoke about in Chapters 1 and 2, "The Importance of Family and Parenting" and "The Importance of Caring." That bothers me greatly, and quite honestly, I'm still trying to figure it all out myself.

FROM A SPEECH TO STUDENTS:

ON EDUCATION

We've all heard it said many times that education is the key to success. I happen to agree with that statement. However, it is important to note that education encompasses and includes many things. In its simplest form, being educated means being literate – in other words, being able to read and write. But in today's high-tech society and global society, education means much more. In addition to being literate, it means being able to understand and comprehend ideas and concepts, it means being able to explain and interpret data and information, it means being able to analyze and synthesize all sorts of information, and it means being able to work cooperatively and collaboratively with others in groups, in teams, and in parts of organizations. It also means being able to discuss issues intelligently, solve problems quickly, and make decisions based on facts and the opinions of many people, including the so-called experts. Being educated today also means being computer savvy, multi-lingual, and being able to navigate this global society successfully.

What we do in school every day is in preparation for the world ahead. I've heard many students say over the years: "What do I need to learn this for?" How is this going to help me?" Here is my answer to that question. Quite honestly, not everything you learn in school will you use in your life. However, what I want you to think about and understand is that learning anything itself is a brain exercise. Your brain, like your body, needs to be exercised regularly. So, although what you may learn in a particular class on a particular day may not be something you will ever use in your lifetime, it is brain training that is taking place, and that alone is worth the exercise.

Education is about acquiring knowledge, learning skills, training your brain, and gaining wisdom. Every day is a day in which we expand and exercise our brain, and in that way we become smarter, more intelligent, and, most importantly, better people. Use each day to learn as much as you can and make each day a worthwhile learning experience.

4
The Importance of Money

Make no mistake about it: Money is important. It may not be the only thing, or the most important thing, but it is very, very important. If you don't think money is important, just ask someone who doesn't have any or doesn't have enough of it. I'm not one of those people who are driven by money or think it's the only thing or the end all. However, the reality is, and I accept this reality, that it is what keeps the economies of the world going, and it is what is needed to provide the resources for people to survive and thrive.

Here's one of the problems: We don't always spend our money wisely and too often we waste it. I don't mind spending money. I do mind wasting money. One of the first things we need to do is understand money and how it works. That may sound simple, but too many people, unfortunately, don't understand it, and we really don't teach it in schools as I think we should. We need to understand it, we need to know why it's important to save it, how to save it, how to spend it wisely, and how to invest it. We also need to hold government accountable for how it uses our money. I am not a believer that government should not spend money. However, again, I don't want government to waste my money. I don't mind paying taxes if the money is used appropriately and wisely. I want my money to be spent on resources that help people and protect our country and its freedoms. I have no problem with that. I do have a problem with spending my money foolishly and wasting it. We need to ensure that our money is spent on education, health care, and safety, including police, fire, and other services that are needed to give all our citizens an opportunity to be successful. I don't understand how we can waste so much money and then say we don't have enough to provide appropriate health care and necessary and essential services for our citizens. That's what government is supposed to do. I know government is complex and bureaucratic, and I know that this is a bit more political than I intended when I started writing; however, it still bothers me.

I also don't quite understand how some people can make so much money and have so much money when others don't have enough or any. Having said that, I am a capitalist. I believe in the capitalist system and I believe that capitalism is one of the reasons that this country, the United States of America, is so great, so successful, and so wealthy. Capitalism provides opportunity. I understand that and I happily accept that. However, somehow we need to equalize the playing field. I believe that business plays a role in all of this as well as government. Somehow we've got to bridge the gap between the haves and the have-nots.

I don't pretend to know the answer. I am, however, presenting the problem or the issue, if you will. I don't even know what is enough money. I guess enough means enough to meet the minimal requirements for survival. What is that? To all of this, quite honestly, I'm still trying to figure it all out myself. But, again, the reality is that money is important, and those who don't have it start way behind those who do have it. And, catching up is often very hard to do (again – not impossible, but difficult).

Let me also make a distinction here in the context of money between "standard of living" and "quality of life." A standard of living to me is how much we have in material things. We often judge (mistakenly, in my opinion) our successes on our standard of living. One may have a big house, or more than one house for that matter, one or more really nice, expensive cars, the best clothes and newest fashions, and the most updated technology. Most people probably have that because they can afford it. They have the money to buy all of those things. A high standard of living does not necessarily guarantee happiness.

Quality of life to me is how much we know, what we do with what we have, and how resourceful we are with the resources we do have, how we develop and grow as individuals, as a family, as a community, and as a society. Quality of life is how happy we are, how much we enjoy our life at the present time, and how optimistic we are about the future. Quality of life also includes our general happiness in life, which is often measured by the relationships and connections we have with other people, especially our family and friends. "Standard of living" and "quality of life" do not always or necessarily go hand-in-hand. They may, but they may not. It is important to remember the difference and it is important for each of us to determine which of the two, if we had to pick one, is more important.

FROM A SPEECH TO STUDENTS:
ON MONEY

I admit that money is important. What I don't agree with is that it should always dictate everything we do and how we make every decision. Money is one of the factors to be taken into account when making a decision. Certainly it would be foolish to dismiss it as a factor. However, when making a decision as to what college to go to, whether to purchase an item or not, etc., one must sometimes look beyond the current cost in the short run to determine if it is the right thing to do or not in the long run. Sometimes we have to sacrifice something now for something in the future. I encourage everyone to respect money, understand its uses and its abuses, and to be smart and intelligent in how we manage it, invest it, save it, and spend it. Like time, money should be spent wisely, not wasted. Finally, it is important and essential to remember that money is a resource, not a determinant in the quality of an individual. Because a person may have more money or less money is in no way indicative of a person's character or integrity. There is no correlation between the two. No one should be judged by the amount of money they have or don't have.

5

The Importance of
Open-Mindedness and Acceptance

The fact that I even have to include this chapter saddens me greatly. We are the United States of America – the land of the free and the home of the brave. I am a proud American of Jewish heritage. My grandparents came to this country to escape the horrors of the pogroms of Russia. My father served our country in World War II, and my brother served in Vietnam. My mother could not get a job with a prominent bank in New York City when she was younger because she was Jewish. My father-in-law was a Holocaust survivor who came to this country after losing his entire family in the camps of Auschwitz and other death camps. I very much appreciate and love this country. In this great nation of ours, open-mindedness should be absolute – a non-issue; acceptance should be part of who we are as a nation. It's what this country was founded on. The fact that I even have to use or mention the terms open-mindedness and acceptance, again, saddens me, but it is what it is.

We are a nation that should not only accept our differences but truly encourage and embrace them. We must respect all races, religions, and ethnic groups. I believe that everyone should be proud of who they are, what their heritage is, and celebrate their cultures. I also believe that we are all Americans, that there is also an American culture that we are all part of and should be part of, and we should celebrate that as well. In addition, we are all world citizens; as such, we should be aware and cognizant of our obligations and responsibilities as world citizens.

Here are some of my issues: Who cares what color our skin is? Do I care what color our hair is? Or our eyes for that matter? So why would I care what color our skin is? Why is that an issue for anyone? Prejudice over skin color is nonsensical and ludicrous. And yet it still exists and I don't get it. People are people. We are all human beings. Everything else about us is the same. We all bleed red, we all have one mouth, one nose, two ears, two eyes, arms, and legs. This obsession about skin color is beyond me. This nonsense needs to stop. I'm not naïve enough to believe that skin color hasn't been or currently isn't an issue. Of course it is. It has been and continues to be a huge issue. I just don't get why it should be. I'm also still trying to figure that one out.

And who cares what religion we are or if we believe or do not believe? Believe what you want or don't believe at all. It doesn't matter to me. Just don't tell me how to believe or what to believe. Please don't push your ideas or beliefs on me. This nation is built on freedom of religion. We do not, nor should we, have an established or official government-sponsored religion. Let us not forget the important concept of the separation of Church and State. This is one of the basic tenets of our Constitution and thereby our political system. And that's okay. That's the way it should be and that's the way I like it. These arguments, battles, and wars over religion are just crazy. It's insanity. Who says that that's okay? Whose God says it's okay to go out and kill others who don't believe as you do? That's not okay. No one should be criticized or persecuted if they believe differently or don't believe at all. That's not freedom of religion. If your God or my God is so good, then why would they want to see other people die in their name? Please answer that one logically. Human beings are making these decisions and interpretations, and this type of prejudice and behavior is totally unacceptable. Let's stop that nonsense.

That takes me to other areas of prejudice and persecution – ethnic background, gender, and sexual orientation, to name a few. Why do I care what ethnic background someone is? We are a nation built by immigrants, those who came here willingly and those who came here against their will. Everyone is welcome here. That's why people come here. They come for the freedoms they can enjoy and for the opportunities that exist. That's the way it should be. We should respect their right to come here and enjoy the comforts of this country just as our ancestors did. Gender wise – obviously women should have the same rights and opportunities as men. That's a given. And they should get the same pay for the same work. For that not to happen is unacceptable. And women should be respected and treated not only fairly but equally and not sexually or otherwise harassed. Sexual orientation – again, who cares? Why is that, like any of the above, an issue?

I am appalled at the prejudices that exist in this world and even in this nation, and I am appalled at how some of us treat each other and act toward one another based on race, religion, ethnic background, gender, and sexual orientation, among other things. I am also appalled at how some people treat different socio-economic classes, as if there is entitlement because someone has more money than another. All of this is beyond unacceptable. We need to get a grip on these prejudices. I'm not exactly sure how; quite honestly, I'm still trying to figure it all out myself.

From a speech to students:
On Open-Mindedness and Acceptance

Personally, I am so impressed by your similarities and differences and by your gifts and talents in so many different areas. I strongly believe that we all learn so much from each other and about each other when we listen, when we observe, when we dialogue, and when we take the time to get to know and understand each other. It's all about communication. It is only through this process of communication that we truly can appreciate each other and respect each other regardless of our racial differences, ethnic backgrounds, religious backgrounds, gender differences, socio-economic differences, sexual orientation, physical appearance, or intellectual ability.

When we take the time to speak to each other and get to know each other, when we listen to each other, we are more apt not to make judgments and we come away with a different viewpoint and perspective rather than making prejudgments based on other people's opinions or on false information gathered or assumed, either by ourselves or others. We should never make assumptions about other people. Get to know people first. Withhold judgment. How easy it is to say hello to someone and ask how he or she is doing, to engage in a conversation with someone, to just be friendly, nice, respectful, and caring to every other person. Making decisions about people prior to knowing them is really what prejudice is.

Prejudice comes from the word pre-judge. Prejudice is not only wrong, it is destructive and dangerous. What normally happens when people are prejudice is that they make decisions based on fears of someone different, someone not like themselves, and/or they have been taught these views by others who are also prejudiced. People are not born prejudiced. They learn it or they are indoctrinated with these views by others. I truly believe that we begin to fight prejudice by respecting each other, accepting each other, and our differences, communicating with each other and making a sincere effort to get to know each other and understand each other.

Again, don't make assumptions. Withhold judgment. It is getting along with all people from all different backgrounds and accepting our differences and our similarities that break down the differences we may have. Of course, we're different. That's the way it should be. How boring it would be if we were all the same. What makes this nation great is our diversity and our differences in not only our backgrounds but in our talents and our skills and abilities. That's why we count on each other, we depend on each other and we don't look at a person's background, racial or ethnic, religious or socio-economic, gender or sexual orientation when we need a service performed or need to purchase something. When we go to a doctor, we want a good, competent physician. We don't care if the doctor is male or female. We don't ask what race he or she is, where their parents are from or what kind of car they drive or where they live or if they're tall, short, heavy, or thin. We want a good, competent doctor. It's interesting that those issues are not issues when we need something done.

To appreciate others, understand others, respect others, to communicate with each other, to not make assumptions, to withhold judgment, and to not be prejudice should be everyone's goal and objective. You never know whom you will need or have to count on one day, and it won't matter to you who they are or where they come from. I will leave you with this quote I wrote:

INTOLERANCE LEADS TO PREJUDICE.
PREJUDICE LEADS TO HATE.
HATE LEADS TO DISCRIMINATION.
DISCRIMINATION LEADS TO PERSECUTION.
PERSECUTION LEADS TO OPPRESSION.
WHEN YOU HAVE OPPRESSION,
EVERYONE'S FREEDOMS ARE IN JEOPARDY.
WHEN THE FIRST STEP HAPPENS,
THE NEXT STEPS SOON FOLLOW.

6
The Importance of
Love

We hear the word love all of the time. Love conquers all. The Beatles said, "All you need is love." We all know it's not all we need but it is something that we all very much need and crave and, too often, don't get enough of. There are many different kinds of love. There is the love for people – our children, our spouses or significant others, our parents, our other family members, our friends. Those are the important loves. There is no love greater than that of a parent for a child – nor should there be (see Chapter 1: "The Importance of Family and Parenting"). There is also self-love or love of ourselves. I've heard it said many times that one cannot love others unless they love themselves also. I don't doubt that this is true. We should definitely have a love and respect for ourselves. I do believe that if we can't love or don't love ourselves, and I don't mean an overbearing, conceited, "I'm so wonderful" type love, but an acceptance of who we are and a likeness for ourselves, then we certainly may have difficulty in sharing our love with others.

We need to like ourselves, give ourselves a break, not expect perfection of ourselves, and to learn to accept our own many strengths and weaknesses, for in that sense we are all truly human. There is also love for things – people love money, art, music, jewelry, clothes, food, sports, among other things. That's a very different kind of love and one that I believe and think needs to be kept in check. When that love of things supersedes the love for people, that's a very big concern for me. Love of people, especially our children – is unconditional. We brought them into this world – we have a responsibility to love them and take care of them. If we don't want to do that, then we shouldn't have children – and that's okay. But when we make that decision, be it planned or in the heat of passion, we should always think before we act – and if we make a child – that becomes our shared re-sponsibility as the mother and the father.

Love means caring deeply about another person (or thing – again, I don't like the "thing" thing), and it means that we would sacrifice almost anything for that individual. It really is putting them even before ourselves. Love is "would we take a bullet for that person?" Love is important because when we love, we care, we make decisions and choices that are in the best interest of those people, and we give of ourselves willingly and selflessly. Never underestimate the power of love. It would be nice to think that the love you give is the love you will receive. It is great to love and it is great to be loved. I don't quite understand how people cannot love at all, and I know that it may have been based on some of their life experiences because I'd like to think that all people are born with the innate ability to love. We need to con-stantly and consistently nourish that.

From a speech to students:
On Love

Good morning. As I was thinking what to write about when it comes to the concept of Love, I said to myself, "Okay, what does love mean to me as an older person, did it always mean the same thing to me, does it mean the same to everyone else, and does it mean the same to younger people like yourselves?" Then I thought, "Isn't love supposed to be a universal word? Doesn't it mean the same to everyone?" I think it does, but I'm not really sure. So, let's talk about it a bit.

To me love means that I deeply care about a person or persons. For example, I love my wife, I love my kids, I loved my parents when they were alive, I love my siblings and their families, I love my friends, I love my career, and I love my students. Yet, as we all know, each of those loves is different and to varying degrees. I'm sure you noticed that except for my career, I mentioned people in that sentence and did not mention things. For example, people might say they love a certain food, or a certain piece of clothing they have, maybe their car or their house. I see a big distinction there. I might like some food, some piece of clothing I have, my car or my house, but if any of those "things" were to disappear or change, it's not like I would feel a tremendous loss or something. I might miss them but I would replace them, if I could. However, people are different. That's love. We don't replace people. We don't just replace a spouse, or a child, or a parent, sibling, or friend. That's a huge *loss. We really miss them when they're gone, and we would sacrifice almost anything to not lose them and to get them back. That's love. Love to me is when we care so deeply that their loss is our loss. Their hurt is our hurt. That's love. People who truly love us genuinely care about us, don't judge us, do support us, encourage us, guide us, and nurture us. They should also be honest with us and truthful with us without being unjustly critical or judgmental. They should also help us and assist us in becoming better people.*

So when we think of love, think of people, think of the people we really and truly care about, think about the people who love us and would do almost anything for us, no questions asked, and think of our ability to care for another person as we would care about ourselves. And always ask ourselves this question: Are the people I love the very same people who also love me? And if that mutual love does truly exist, then they are truly worthy of our time, our energy, our sacrifices, whatever they may be, our trust and respect, and our continuous affection. That's love.

7

The Importance of Respect, Self-Respect, and Self-Confidence

Respect comes in many forms. Respect implies that we value and show consideration for other people. It is the utmost compliment to another person when we respect them and the utmost compliment to ourselves when others respect us. Successful relationships are built upon respect and trust. Self-respect is how we think of ourselves, because how we think of ourselves will often determine how other people think of us as well; even more importantly, how we think of ourselves will help shape our happiness and success.

As people we, again, have our many strengths and weaknesses. We know that and we work to build upon our strengths and to improve upon our weaknesses. Sometimes we need to accept that there are just some things we are not very good at. That should not mean that we have a low opinion of ourselves and give up. It does mean that we may possibly redirect our focus and our time and energy on the things we do well. Self-confidence is our ability to accept ourselves with our frailties and move on to do what we need to do, deal with the challenges that occur in life, and begin to work through those challenges successfully.

It is essential that we always show respect for others, that we respect ourselves, and that we maintain our self-confidence while facing the many challenges of life itself. With self-respect and self-confidence, we are more apt to meet those challenges successfully.

FROM A SPEECH TO STUDENTS:
ON RESPECT

Respect is demonstrated by how we treat others. Respect is demonstrated by how we treat ourselves – that is, of course, self-respect. Respect is showing regard for all people regardless of who they are, what they look like, where they come from, what they do for a living, how much money they have or don't have. Respect is appreciating the contributions of all members of our society. Respect comes from within our hearts and is shown and demonstrated in our treatment of others through our words, actions, attitudes, and body language. All relationships, be they personal (family member to family member, friend to friend) or be they professional relationships (teacher and student, parent and school, school and community), all begin and maintain themselves through respect. No matter where you are or what you're doing, treat everyone with the utmost respect and dignity at all times. Also, don't forget to respect yourself. Respect is the cornerstone of any and all relationships.

FROM A SPEECH TO STUDENTS:
ON HOW WE TREAT OTHERS

How we treat each other at all times is often determined by our feelings, our thoughts, our principles and values, and sometimes even by our moods. Moods are a temporary state of mind while thoughts, feelings, principles, and values are more of a permanent state, an attitude, if you will. These thoughts, feelings, and principles guide our attitudes, which in turn guide our words, behaviors, and actions. We always need to be aware of how these words, behaviors, and actions impact other people. We need to be careful in what we say, how we say it, how we behave, and how we act at all times. And that always comes back to respect. We need to always be aware of how we treat other people, and we should always remember the golden rule: Treat others as you yourself would like to be treated.

From a speech to students:
On Self-Confidence and Peer Pressure

I have a couple of questions for you: Do you sometimes wonder what other people might think of you? Do you ever say to yourself, what will my friends say or think if I choose to do something or I choose not to do something? Do you sometimes maybe feel a bit insecure, lack some self-confidence, feel peer pressure, and sometimes make decisions you really didn't want to make or later regret because of the peer pressure or fear that the group won't accept you? Well, unfortunately, you are not alone! Many of us, if not most of us, are all, admittedly, a bit insecure at some points in our lives, or at least have been in some situations, and many of us work hard every day to fight those insecurities and fears. How do we do that? We do that by building up our self-confidence, by focusing in on what we do right, by looking at the positives, by learning from our mistakes, and by always trying to do our very best in everything we do. We also do that by learning from others, observing others, listening to others, and building our own knowledge base, skill levels, and wisdom. And most of all, we do that by looking into our own conscience and making decisions as to what is right and what is wrong.

Today I'd like to discuss with you self-confidence, fear of non-acceptance, insecurity, and peer pressure because I think they are all so very important in defining who you and I are as people – and all those words and/

or concepts overlap and are really tied together. The reason why I say that is because I believe that when people lack self-confidence or are insecure, they are more apt to give in to peer pressure. They may do things because they want to be accepted. I have news for you again: We all want to be accepted. That's a normal human desire and need. We all want to feel that we belong, that we are liked, that we are appreciated and respected, that our friends will remain our friends, but we also need to know that our friends have to respect us as individuals and respect our decisions, and we need to stand up for ourselves. That, again of course, is assuming that our own decisions are the right ones.

I would venture to guess that we all want people to like us. We all want friends. We all want to be part of a group. But the need to be accepted or belonging or being liked should never supersede or overshadow our giving in to peer pressure and doing some thing or some things that may seem cool at the time but are really foolish and maybe even very unwise. When we give in to peer pressure, I believe that the decisions we are making are not our own but are rather influenced by what others think we should do or talk us into doing. And I don't think that people who pressure us into doing things that we're really not comfortable doing are truly looking out for our best interests or are our real and true friends. When we give in when we know we shouldn't, it is often reflected in our lack of self-confidence and our insecurities. Some people do things because others do it. By having self-confidence, by being secure in who we are, by having the ability to believe in ourselves, the ability to be reassured by our own ideas, actions, and values, the ability to trust ourselves in our own judgment and in making our own decisions and in making our own choices, we take control. When we take control we begin to have the trust, the assurance, the belief, and the faith in our own abilities to do the right things and not to be influenced by the choices and decisions of others that we don't agree with or are not comfortable with.

When it comes to peer pressure, that's when our own confidence has to take over and ensure that we take control and not give in. My rule of thumb is this: Do what you think is right and don't care what other people think as long as you know in your heart that you're right and comfortable with what you're doing. That's all that really counts. Don't be influenced by the actions or choices of others to do anything you don't want to do. Take responsibility for your actions, your decisions, and your choices. Don't blame others for what you choose to do or choose not to do. That's where self-confidence comes in. Your responsibility is to make your own choices and to always be in control of your own behavior and actions. Under no circumstances does the will of the group supersede your own will to make your own decisions and choices. Never let another person dictate your behavior. You always want to be aware of what you are doing and why. You always want to be in control of yourself. So, always have confidence in yourself, and when you do you become less insecure be-

cause you have developed a sense of trust in yourself, a confidence, and a belief in yourself and assurance and spirit that permeates your entire being. With peer pressure, never, ever, let another person or group of people dictate to you what to do or influence your actions, especially if in your heart, if in your gut, you know it's not the right thing. You don't impress people by caving in; then they are in control. You impress people, and even more than that you impress yourself, when you make the decisions and you're in control. The ability to make your own decisions and choices and not be influenced by the negative peer pressures of others takes lots of self-confidence and self-respect.

Let me tell you your real rights: You have a right to say no. You have a right to say stop. You have a right to say that you're not doing something that you're not comfortable with doing, you have a right to leave. You have the right to be in control of your own behavior and actions. And you always have the right to make your own choices and decisions. You have a right to be in control. If you give that up, that's your choice and you have to live with the results and implications, and you can't blame others for what you do. If your friends or the people you're with do not respect your decisions or choices, assuming of course that you are making good choices, then question their friendship. If giving in to peer pressure is what it takes to be accepted or liked, you need to move on to a different group of people who accept you for who you are and for what you believe in. Quite frankly, good friends will respect you for what you stand up for. If not, you may need to look elsewhere. And remember the quote:"What is right is not always popular and what is popular is not always right."

8

The Importance of
Character and Integrity

C haracter is more important than intelligence. I've heard
this saying many times. Being smart and intelligent tells
us nothing about our character and integrity. Nothing
is more important or speaks more about us as a person than our
character and integrity. It is truly who we are as a person. It is
how we act, how we behave, how we treat others, at all times.
Character is sometimes referred to as how one acts and behaves
when no one is looking or watching. People with character and
integrity are fair, respectful, honest, and trustworthy. These are
people you trust. These are the people that we have the utmost
faith and confidence in and the people we can always count on.
They are true to themselves and they are true to others. If everyone had character and integrity, what a really nice place the world
would be. People with character and integrity live by their words
and through their actions. I've always believed that other people
can take a lot away from a person, but they can't take away their
character, integrity, and self-respect.

When others are looking for a person to be a friend, to hire
for a job, to watch and care for their children, to do business
with, and to build a relationship with, they will always look for
a person with character and integrity. I believe that if there were

only two traits that people have that are most important and most significant, it would be their character and integrity. Our character and integrity really demonstrate what kind of people we really are.

I've seen and used this quote many times:

Watch your thoughts;
they become words.

Watch your words;
they become actions.

Watch your actions;
they become habits.

Watch your habits;
they become your character.

Watch your character;
it becomes your destiny.

by Frank Outlaw

From a speech to students:
On Character and Integrity

Often times in our lives we come into contact with people who possess two very important characteristics: Character and Integrity. These are the people who do things for the right reasons. These are the people who are honest and sincere. They treat people respectfully and fairly, they are trustworthy and caring, and they always act and behave with the utmost class and dignity. These are the people other people seek to be with. These are the people that set the standards for behavior and performance. They do good deeds, they conduct themselves in a professional manner, and they are responsible, dependable, and reliable.

How does one acquire character and integrity? I believe that some of it is inherent and much of it is learned from our parents, our teachers, our coaches, advisors, counselors, and other role models. They are qualities that we have to want to become part of who we are, and we need to demonstrate those qualities in our actions and behaviors on a daily basis. It means being unselfish, accepting, collegial, cooperative, and unwavering in our values, morals, and ethical behavior. It is living and behaving within the standards of right and wrong. Maintaining our character and integrity throughout our lives is truly one of the most important and respected traits and characteristics each of us can ever possess. I encourage all of us to aspire to a life of character and integrity.

9

The Importance of Responsibility and Following Through

A key cornerstone to living in a society, especially a free society, is taking responsibility for ourselves and our actions, behaviors, and attitude. There really is no excuse to shift that responsibility to others. We can't blame others for our choices and our decisions in life. The ultimate person responsible for us is us. In addition, it is important that we adults live up to our responsibilities by taking care of our family and our children and teaching them to grow up and be responsible and productive members of society.

Being responsible means being accountable to ourselves and to others. It is following through on our commitments, our word, our promises to ourselves and to others. Every one of us relies and depends on other people every day. It is essential that we take our responsibilities seriously and understand that if we do not fulfill our responsibilities, we impact our own lives as well as the lives of others, especially those who put their trust and confidence in us. It is disappointing and disconcerting when people are not responsible and don't follow through on what they say they are going to do. Again, we can't blame others for our choices and our decisions. Responsibility is a key component to living a happy and successful life. Other people trust, respect, admire, and look up to responsible people.

FROM A SPEECH TO STUDENTS:
ON RESPONSIBILITY

Yes, the actions and behaviors of others hurt sometimes even innocent people. We all have a responsibility to act responsibly in everything we do and in the decisions we make. Sometimes our actions are harmful to us, sometimes they are harmful to others, and sometimes they are harmful to both others and ourselves. We need to always be in control of our actions and be aware and cognizant of the decisions we are making and the actions we are taking.

Responsibility wears many hats. Being responsible means that we're dependable, reliable, and trustworthy and that we're going to do what we say we're going to. In other words, following through on our word. Following through and living up to our commitments, including accomplishing the tasks we have set for ourselves. Doing our homework, studying for tests, doing chores at home, reaching our goals, and living up to our duties and obligations are all part of responsibility.

Responsibility also means using good judgment and making decisions that take into account how our actions and behaviors will affect and impact not only ourselves but also others. Responsibility is being accountable for our actions. Responsibility is not about blaming others. Responsible people accept blame when they make mistakes, they learn from their mistakes, they correct their mistakes, and they always look to use good judgment and make good decisions that are in the best interest of everyone, not just themselves.

Responsible people are the ones we can count on. They are the people who we put our trust in, who we put our faith in, who we put our confidence in, sometimes even who we trust our lives with. This is Prom weekend. Whether you're going or not is not important. What is important is that I implore each and every one of you to please act responsibly, as I hope you always do, prom or not, using good judgment and making good choices and good decisions. As you know every Friday I end my announcements with "Come back to us safely on Monday." To tell you the truth, to me that is actually the most important thing I say to you every Friday. I say that for a reason. I will continue to say that every Friday because I care about you; we all care about you, and we all should care about each other. To me, that's the most important thing – caring about each other and being healthy and safe. I want you to always remember that, think that, say that to others, believe that, live that, and do everything you can, everything in your power to make sure that you come back to us safely on Monday – and every day.

I am going to trust that you will be responsible, behave responsibly, and live up to your responsibilities and – come back to us safely on Monday. We do care. Have a great day.

FROM A SPEECH TO STUDENTS:
ON FOLLOWING THROUGH

One of the many things I say at the end of my announcements is: follow through on your commitments in both your personal life and professional life. As I was thinking about that I remembered my father telling me as a young boy, "Son, people don't want excuses, they want results. Make sure you follow through." That has stuck with me throughout my entire life. People are not interested in why we didn't do something; they are disappointed, frustrated, and maybe even angry when we don't follow through on what we said we were going to do or on what we promised. And they may be right in their feelings. We may have a very good excuse for not following through, but "people don't want excuses, they want results."

We've all heard that "talk is cheap." Talk is cheap only when it is not followed by action. When we say we're going to do something, when we make a commitment, when we make a promise, to ourselves or to someone else, it is our obligation and our responsibility to take action and follow through on that commitment. That's part of living up to our responsibilities. Our WORD is our character. It helps determine our trust factor. People expect us to follow through on our word. They count on us. If we say we're going to do something, or be somewhere, we need to follow through on that. Everybody has good intentions, or at least, I'd like to think so. It is those people who follow through that are successful, and it is those people that we can count on. Following through also entails following through on our own promises to ourselves. It is not only a commitment to others to follow through; it is a commitment to ourselves.

FROM A SPEECH TO STUDENTS:
ON FOLLOWING THROUGH, PART II

Like it or not, people judge us. And, they judge us by our words, our actions, our attitude, our behaviors, and our work ethic, how we treat others, and our commitment and follow through. Our reputations are based on it. So is our legacy. When we say we're going to do something, we need to do it. When we make a promise, we need to keep it. When we give our word, we need to follow through on it. And when we make a commitment, we need to stick to it. This includes not only those commitments to other people, but also those commitments and promises we make to ourselves. Both are so important. When we follow through, people respect us, know we are responsible individuals, and know that we're a person they can count on and a person of our WORD. When we make a commitment to ourselves and follow through, we know that our determination and pride will ensure that we keep our word to ourselves. We shouldn't make promises or commitments to ourselves or others that we can't keep, may not be able to keep, or have no intention of keeping. "People don't want excuses, they want results." Be responsible. Follow through.

10
The Importance of Relationships

L ife is all about relationships, positive relationships. Relationships with other people, the connections we make,
the associations we have with others, the need for human
contact, and the interactions we have are so very important in
all of our lives. It is our dealings with people that make us who
we are. It is those relationships and connections that make life
worthwhile. Things don't really make us happy, at least in the
long run. They may for a short while, but after a time, things become "old" and we want something newer and bigger to fill our
needs and wants. Things are short lasting and really unfulfilling.
Relationships with people are different. They are ongoing, they
get stronger over the years, there is dialogue, conversation, and
exchange of ideas and thoughts, experiences and stories, many of
which we tell over and over again and never get tired of. That's
the fun part. To get together and socialize, to laugh and have fun,
to enjoy each other's company; that's truly what is important.

Relationships also provide a forum for family and friends
to talk and confide in each other, to help and assist each other,
to encourage and support each other. What better way to live a
fulfilled life than to build on positive relationships with family
and friends?

FROM A SPEECH TO STUDENTS:
ON FRIENDSHIP

Today I'd like to discuss with you one of the most important relationships we have in our lives with other people – and that is friendship. What does it really mean to be a friend? And a good friend at that? I think outside of one's family, our friends are probably the most important people in our lives. Some of us have many friends; some of us have a few friends. Hopefully, everyone has at least one or two good friends or some good friends. A friend is defined as a person whom one knows, likes, and trusts. In many ways, I guess that says it all. I think we all want to have friends. I think we all like to be a friend to others. I think we all need friends. We need friends to share things with and to share time with, and we want friends to go places with, to talk with, and dare I say to hang out with. We also need friends to support us, care about us, guide us, encourage us, and stand by us. Having said all that, we also all know that friends have a very important influence on us, but I must say here that that influence must be a positive influence and not a negative influence. Choose your friends very carefully.

Trust and respect are the cornerstones of friendship. We need to know that our friends do trust us, do respect us, and do truly care about us. Friends are people who will stand by us and support us, not only in the good times, but also, most importantly, during our most difficult and challenging times. Friends listen to us, friends watch out for us and want the best for us, as we do for them. Friends are not jealous of us or of our successes. Friends are selfless, unselfish people, friends give us good and positive advice, friends sacrifice for us, friends help us problem-solve, and friends don't abandon us. Most importantly, good friends don't judge us. Those are our true and real friends.

It is quite possible that over the years your friends may change. You will most likely gain some and you may possibly lose some for various reasons. (I am very fortunate to still have many friends from my early childhood, four to be exact, one pretty much from the day I was born, Kenny, and three from elementary school – Alan, Alan, and Gerry, and we all know how long ago that was. I am still very friendly with all four of them today. I also have friends from high school, college and my years working.) However, I will tell you that we all have to work hard at it to maintain friendships over many years. Like any relationship, it takes work, time, and energy.

Do not use the term "friend" lightly. When we call someone a friend, we are giving them one of the biggest compliments we can, and with that friendship comes a tremendous responsibility for both of us. At this point we have taken each other into our inner circle, into our trust and confidence, into our lives. It is important that we have good friends, and it is important that we are good friends to each other. One of those responsibilities is when we see a friend in trouble or in need, and this goes for us adults as well as kids, we need to make sure that we do whatever is absolutely necessary to help that individual. Sometimes that means letting another responsible adult know, or a person who is in the position to help, so that the help and support that is needed for the friend is provided. Ignoring a problem never helps solve it and may even lead to other, more serious problems and issues later on. We must act when someone, especially a friend, is in distress. That is one of our responsibilities and obligations of being a friend. And friends don't let friends do foolish stuff.

A special message now to my senior friends on friendship and your next couple of weeks in high school – and everyone needs to hear this also because you will all be in this position one day real soon. I know that all of you seniors are very anxious to graduate and move on. I understand that. I know that you're excited, as well you should be, about the upcoming events that will culminate with graduation in June. I encourage you to enjoy your remaining 6 weeks or so here in high school with your friends and classmates, some of whom you will continue to be friends with and will see again, some of whom you may not see again as often, and some of whom you may never see again, except at a reunion or by happening to run into them at some point in the future.

Enjoy these last few weeks here with each other for you will never have these high school days again. Have fun, but continue to be careful and be safe. That's a given and, of course, that goes for everyone.

Seniors: Your days as high schoolers are quickly coming to an end, but your hopes for the future are just beginning. Keep the positive friendships and relationships alive – and that has a double meaning – alive as in well and good and alive as in living and survival like I talked about last time. Have fun, but please be careful and be safe.

11
The Importance of
Attitude and Good Habits

I have heard this many times over the years: Aptitude + Attitude = Altitude. I believe it to be very true. Again, Aptitude, our ability, plus Attitude, our demeanor, our way of behaving and acting, our manner and our approach to situations and life in general, equals Altitude, how far we will go in life. I truly believe that one of the keys to a happy and successful life is our own attitude, and there is only one person that controls that on a daily basis, and that is us. We can blame others, we can blame situations, and we can give excuses for things, but in the end, each of us decides how to behave and act on a daily basis, how we will treat other people, and how we react to others and to situations and circumstances.

Our attitude is our approach to things, our way of behaving on a daily basis. Our attitude comes through in our words and in our actions. It comes through verbally and non-verbally. Sometimes we can just tell a person's attitude by how they carry themselves, their expressions, how they act, how they behave, and how they treat others. We can sense it. It's comforting when dealing with someone with a good attitude, and it's very uncomfortable when dealing with someone who has a poor attitude.

I very rarely have seen someone with a poor attitude be successful or liked. However, I've seen many people with good attitudes who have not only been successful but have been liked and admired as well.

FROM A SPEECH TO STUDENTS:
ON ATTITUDE

Today I want to discuss what I think is one of the most important words and concepts in our lives, and if we get this going in the right direction, there is nothing that will stop any of us from being successful. We've heard the word before – it's not a new word, but I want us to think about it and reflect on it every time we interact with others. That word is ATTITUDE. Any time we interact with someone, we convey or display an attitude, how we act, and how we behave. It is our total being. It is a reflection of who we are. If it's positive, we reap the rewards. If it's negative, we often suffer the consequences. Our attitude is how we carry ourselves, how we perceive life, and how we confront life and its many challenges and issues, how we act in life on a daily basis, how we react to situations and circumstances, some of which may be out of our control, how we behave, what we say, how we say it, and what we do and how we do it. Our attitude is displayed in our words and actions every day, every minute, every second.

We all know people who have what we call a "bad attitude." They are often not real comfortable to be around, and not people we want to hang out with for the most part. Those with good attitudes are comfortable to be around, fun to be with, and look at life as the glass being half full instead of half empty. This is not to say that we don't sometimes get into bad moods, get angry, get stressed, or get frustrated; I'm as guilty as anyone else in this area. But those moods should only be temporary. We need to appropriately deal with that anger, that stress, those frustrations, resolve the issues, and move on. But our general demeanor, how we act most of the time, how we interact with other people, how we look at life, and how we treat others and ourselves should always be positive. If respect is the main cornerstone of relationships, then a good, positive attitude is the main determinant and ingredient for success, and a bad, poor attitude will probably or inevitably lead to a lack of success. I encourage all of us to do attitude checks, daily if need be, and see if the attitude we have, the attitude we display to others, is truly the one we want to have. A good attitude becomes a habit.

I encourage all of us to have a positive attitude, and I believe that if we develop a positive attitude and maintain a positive attitude, we will be happier and more successful in life. And remember, our attitudes are contagious. When we have a positive attitude, we exude and convey positive attitudes to others as well.

I will leave you with something I've heard a couple of times that I suspect may be true: 90% of people lose their jobs or get fired not because they are not good at what they do or are incompetent, but because they can't get along with other people or have a poor or bad attitude. If we want to be the best at what we do, let us start with a good, positive attitude every day. Remember, our daily attitude is a choice, and that is always within our control. We choose what to say, how to say it, how to act and behave, and how to treat others.

FROM A SPEECH TO STUDENTS:
ON WORK ETHIC AND ATTITUDE

Two things in particular are often responsible for one's success or lack thereof in whatever we do. Those two things are our work ethic and our attitude. Our work ethic is how we approach what we have to get done. How well do we do it? How much effort do we put into it? Our attitude is how we approach life in general and how we view the world, how we view others, and how we view ourselves. Our attitude is written all over us by our non-verbal cues and actions and by our words and how we approach others. In summary, I would recommend that we always do our very best and we always put forth our best efforts. Another couple of hints: Get things done early. Don't wait till the last minute. Don't procrastinate. No last-minute stuff. Get off to a good start. Create good habits from the beginning, and then your work ethic becomes second nature.

FROM A SPEECH TO STUDENTS:
ON FEAR OF FAILURE

Today I want to discuss with you both a word and a concept that often dictates our actions, influences our decisions, monopolizes our thoughts, and probably stresses us out more often than we need to be stressed and more often than we think. That word and concept is fear.

As human beings we may have some fears. But the fear I really want to talk to you about today is a fear that many of us, if not all of us currently have or have had at one point in our lives, including myself: the fear of failure. Rule #1: Failure, or as I prefer to call it, "temporary setbacks," will occur in all of our lives at some point unless, of course, we never try to succeed at anything. Rule #2: we can't change Rule #1. I never met anyone who never failed at something, unless of course they never tried to do anything. Fear of failure exists because we never want to admit to ourselves or anyone else that we are not or were not successful at something we attempted or tried. Fear of failure often dictates and drives our decisions, our actions, our behaviors, and our attitudes.

If we fear failure, then we don't try or explore new things or try to do something that is challenging because we fear failing and not being successful. So we avoid it at all costs. Somehow when we fail at something, our confidence, which is often fragile anyhow, is shattered. I understand that, but I don't agree with it.

In fact, it should be just the opposite. Our confidence level should be elevated because we tried. If all things were easy, then anyone could do them. What makes each and every one of us special and unique is our abilities to do different things well. If we did everything well, we'd all be perfect. And remember, none of us is perfect. And if we all did the same things well, then we'd all be the same and end up the same. And we're not. That's why there are doctors, engineers, teachers, mechanics, nurses, architects and hairdressers, computer people and athletes, artists and musicians, and the list goes on and on. Instead of not trying and fearing failure when we're having difficulty with something or struggling with something, we need to be able to admit it and say: "I'm having trouble with this issue or problem, or I'm having trouble or difficulty understanding this concept or this idea, but I'm going to try anyhow. Can you help me?" It's okay to ask for help. Asking for help is not a sign of weakness. Quite the contrary. It is a sign of courage and strength to ask for help.

We all need to face our fear of failure or it will haunt us for the rest of our lives. Once we can overcome our fear of failure, again, because we're not perfect, our chances for success will increase significantly. Work to overcome your fear of failure because there is no shame in failure if you are trying the very best you can. There is only shame in not trying. And, I can tell you this: you're not going to be the first person to fail at something you try, and you're not going to be the last person to fail at something you try. But you never want to be that person who never tries because those who try are those who succeed, and those who succeed have failed at some things and at some points in their lives, if not many things. But they never gave up, and they never gave in to the fear of failure. The last time I spoke with you, I said no one is a "loser." Well, no one is a failure. The only failure, again, is in not trying. I would say that the number one reason why some people are not successful is fear of failure. The key to our success will be in our ability to maintain confidence in our abilities and ourselves and to bounce back and recover from our setbacks. Successful people do not allow failures, defeats, or setbacks to stop them from following their road to success. In fact, it often makes successful people even more determined to succeed.

The difference between those people who succeed and those who do not is not necessarily their differences in ability; rather, it is in their belief and confidence that they will not let the inevitable setbacks that they will or may confront or face stop their determination and desire for their desired goals. The old adages, "if at first you don't succeed, try and try again," and, "never give up," are as true today as they ever were. The only thing that will defeat us in life is our attitude and not believing in ourselves, and that is always within our control. Have confidence in yourself and your skills and abilities. And as you've heard me say many times before, our skills and abilities may not be the same as everybody else's, but we all have them in some area. Fear of failure is not a reason not to try. Success is never guaranteed, but confidence and belief in ourselves and our abilities, as well as a good positive attitude, will allow us to keep moving forward towards success. And though there may very well be some failures, or should I say setbacks along the way, we have the power and control to overcome them. If we have no fear of failure, we will always challenge ourselves to do things we never thought we would or could do or were possible.

FROM A SPEECH TO STUDENTS:
ON WORK ETHIC

What I would like to do today is briefly talk with you about a concept that will truly determine your success, both at school and in life in general. That concept is called our work ethic. What do I mean by our work ethic? Simply stated, it is the attitude we bring to our work, to our education, to our recreational activities (be it our team or group or anything else we're involved in or with or part of), to our life in general. It is our attitude, our habits, our mindset, our way of doing things. The question becomes: Do we always look to do the best we can in everything we do? Or do we look to do as little as possible and to get away with as much as we can? These are huge questions, and our answers to those two questions will truly determine our work ethic and our attitude, and it will show in our performance in whatever we do or are involved in. The answer to those questions will be the difference between our success and failure.

We must always care about what we're doing and always give 100%, whether it's in the classroom, at the job, on the field, or during a performance. Whatever it is, less than 100% is not acceptable. That's our work ethic. And if we're not giving everything our best shot, we're only fooling and hurting ourselves. Our work ethic is an attitude, it's a mindset, it's habit, and it's a lifestyle. I will tell you that if your work ethic is not where it should be, you need to change it now.

I believe that the only thing that will stop any of us from being successful in life, more than anything else, will not be our lack of ability because, as I've said to you many times before, each and every one of us has an ability to do not just one thing, but many things very well. What will stop us will be our lack of effort, our lack of initiative, dare I say the "laziness factor." More than anything else, what has stopped people from being successful has been a poor attitude, a lack of effort, a lack of initiative, a lack of trying, a poor work ethic, procrastination, and just plain laziness. Don't let that happen to you. We must always put forth our best efforts in everything we do and try the hardest we can at every thing we do, especially our schoolwork. That's a major part of the formula for success. And if we always do the things we have to do and make the effort and have the work ethic, we'll almost always be able to do the things we want to do and enjoy to do. How well we practice will also determine how well we will perform.

I would encourage all of us to make whatever changes are necessary in our actions, behaviors, attitudes, and habits that will bring us the success we desire for ourselves. The opportunity is always there for us to commit ourselves to success. We need to have confidence in ourselves and our abilities, have pride in what we do, and let people help us succeed. We need to become better students, better people, better friends, every day. We need to improve, even if just a little bit upon the day before. After all, isn't that what it's all about? To be smarter, wiser, nicer, more successful, than we were the day before? Every day is a new beginning and a new opportunity for each of us to do something better, to do something different, and to do something great.

12
The Importance of
Good Communication
and Good Listening

How many times have we all heard these statements? If we could or would only communicate effectively with one another.... If I would have known what you were thinking.... If you would have told me.... If you would have let me know. Unfortunately, we hear these all too often. What does it really mean to communicate, and what does it really mean to communicate effectively? First of all, communication comes in many forms, most notably verbal and non-verbal, and both are very significant. We must always be aware of what we say and how we say it. We also must be very aware of our body language and the vibes we give off. Our body speaks volumes: the way we sit, the way we stand, the way we move our head, arms, and hands, and the way we look at each other. Our mouth says words, but our body speaks just as loudly.

Verbal communication means to exchange and share ideas, thoughts, and information. It also means speaking and listening, discussing, conversing, and dialoguing, questioning, and answering. It also means keeping each other and others informed. Again, how many times have I heard the excuse that we just didn't communicate effectively, if at all? Communication has to take place in the home, between parents themselves, between parents and children, between or among siblings, and between other extended family. Communication has to take place in all aspects of our lives. In school it is among teachers, parents, and students and other school or family personnel. In the workplace it is among employers and employees, management and union. Teams communicate on the field and on the court all of the time. Orchestras and bands communicate. Performers communicate with each other. When they don't communicate, mistakes occur. People can't read our minds. We have to somehow – orally, in writing, and non-verbally – express ourselves clearly. Our ability to communicate in this world will have a tremendous impact on our ability to be successful. Good communication will help us in everything we do. Poor communication will always create problems for us. Never forget the importance of good communication. Never assume that other people know what you're thinking or understand what you're saying. If you don't understand, ask. If you think others don't understand you, ask. Let's try and make sure that we always try to have constant and consistent communication with all of the people we deal with on both a personal and professional basis. It will not only save us time and aggravation, it will keep us knowledgeable and aware.

It is also very important to be aware of and remember that good communication also entails effective listening. Communication is not just about "the communicator," the person speaking or doing the communicating. It is also very much about "the communicatee" – the listener. In order to communicate with others effectively, we must be willing to listen effectively. Listening entails focusing, concentrating, understanding, and giving our full attention to the person or persons doing the communicating and to what is being communicated, how it is being communicated, and why it is being communicated.

In this new and modern age of electronic communication, through email, texting, etc., I think it is also important to remember and try to follow the very same guidelines of good communication, basically ensuring that the "sender" communicates effectively and clearly and that the "receiver" listens well and understands the message.

From a speech to students: On Communication

Mark Twain said, "If God wanted us to talk more than listen, he (or she) would have given us two mouths and one ear." Having said that, both skills are really important. We must learn to listen and listen carefully, intently, and sensitively, but we must also learn to talk and communicate clearly, concisely, effectively, and appropriately.

I would venture to say that most problems that exist among people are caused by miscommunication and can be resolved through good communication. And I stress "most," not "all." Too often we don't listen to what is being said because we are so intent on talking and speaking and getting our point across that we neglect to allow the other person or persons to speak, so that they can get their point(s) across. There may be times when some issues are not resolved, but there will be more times that they will be resolved if everyone stops, really listens, fully digests what the other person is saying, and reacts appropriately in a non-threatening, non-judgmental manner.

    Personal attacks are not an appropriate way to communicate. We can disagree on ideas, thoughts, or philosophies, but we should never personally attack another person's viewpoint assuming that they are rational and within reason. (My point is that people with prejudice or hateful views would be an exception to this rule.) Ladies and Gentlemen: Always try to become good communicators both verbally and non-verbally. What will help all of us be successful in anything we do will be our ability to effectively communicate with all people, and that includes having good listening and good verbal skills.

13
The Importance of Time

The clock keeps ticking. It never, ever stops. It doesn't stop for me and it doesn't stop for you. Time comes and time goes. And the older we get, the quicker it seems to go. It seems like only yesterday that I was a kid. I like to use this baseball analogy: When I was a kid, I was in the dugout, my parents were in the on-deck circle and my grandparents were at bat. My grandparents and parents are long gone. I'm up. I'm at bat. Some times that's pretty scary, but that's how it goes. Quite honestly, I'm still glad I'm here. I'm happy to be alive. Like I may have said before, "If I wake up, it's a good day."

A couple of thoughts about time: Thought #1: Time is very precious. Enjoy the time you spend with your family and friends. The *Happy Days* character Arthur Fonzarelli, better known as Fonzie or The Fonz, said to a group of parents who were attending a high school play for their kids in one of the show's episodes, "You better dig what you have now because you ain't gonna have it forever." How true that is. Cherish your time with people. Enjoy yourself and don't wish your life away.

Thought #2: Be respectful of time – your time and the time of others. In our society, people get paid for their time; it's often called their labor. Basically it's their time of doing something for someone for a fee. Make sure that you are aware of time, and when you have an appointment or a place to be at a certain time, be there on time or early. It is disrespectful and inconsiderate to be late for an appointment.

Again, be aware and respectful or your time and other people's time. Time is the only resource that cannot be accumulated or saved. Time is to spend, not to waste.

FROM A SPEECH TO STUDENTS:
ON TIME

There are very few things in this life that are exactly the same for all of us. In almost everything I can think of, there is a difference. We all come in different sizes, shapes, colors, and backgrounds. We all, as I've said before, have different talents, gifts, strengths, and weaknesses. We all do things differently, say things differently, interpret things differently; we have different tastes in food, clothing, movies, books, television shows, music, subjects, and even people, friends for that matter. If anything, all these differences make us all stronger, more interesting and varied, as it should be. However, there is one thing that we all have that is exactly the same. And we all have an equal amount of it every day, yet none of us knows how long we will have it for. When it comes to that, the future, we are all shooting in the dark. It's a guessing game at best. The concept I am talking about is TIME. Yes, we all have the same 24 hours a day/7 days a week. None of us has more and none of us has less.

Time is the great equalizer. It doesn't matter what our size, shape, color, or background is. It doesn't matter if we are rich or poor, young or old, big or little, our daily time is always the same. Time is the great equalizer. What will not be equal is how much of that time we have in our lives. That's up for grabs. However, those 24 hours a day is the time allotted to each one of us on a daily basis. What we choose to accomplish in any given day, how we choose to spend that time, use that time, dare I say waste that time, is totally up to us for the most part. Certainly there are things we have to do: sleep, eat, go to school, go to work, do homework, do some chores, and there are some things we like to do, go out with our friends and socialize, play and/or listen to music, play and/or watch sports, spend time on our interests and hobbies, whatever they may be. How much time we devote to the things we have to do and want to do is often up to us, and the reality is, as we get older, we may get more choices on how we utilize our time.

Last week I said that the past is the past and it never comes back. The time we have spent or wasted, the time we have used, is gone forever. Hopefully, we've spent lots more time than we've wasted. Time is not infinite. That means it is not forever. So, how we spend the time we have is crucial to our success, our happiness and our futures. The time we invest now in the present, being successful in school, learning skills, increasing our knowledge base, gaining wisdom, learning to get along with others, treating others respectfully, maintaining a positive attitude, will allow us to have more choices in how we spend our time in the future. We all want control of our time.

The best way to get that is to use our time wisely now so that it can be used appropriately and wisely later. Time is ongoing, time is valuable, and, again, time is the only thing we all have the same of every day. Time is our most valuable resource.

Again, once it is used it is gone forever. How we choose to use it and whom we choose to spend it with are some of our most important decisions on a daily basis. I suggest that we all wisely use those 24 hours given to us and that we treat time as a very precious gift that is to be respected and utilized to the best of our abilities. I will leave you with a well-known quote: "It's not what time does to us, it's what we do with time," and, once again, like our attitude, that's almost always our choice and within our control.

14
The Importance of
Being Nice and Being Kind

I am always impressed with nice and kind people. I think the best compliment we can give to someone is to say that they are nice and kind. One wonders, why some people are so nice and kind and others – let's just say, not so? Are people born nice and kind, do they learn it, or do they make a conscious effort to be that way? I'm not sure but I would venture to say that it's a combination of all those things. I'm pretty certain modeling has a lot to do with it. Unfortunately, I guess it's the same for people who are not so nice and kind; however, the question becomes, do they make a conscious effort to be not nice, unkind, and perhaps even cruel and mean?

Unfortunately, there are mean people. You know there are and I know there are. I don't know why and I certainly don't know what joy and happiness they get from being that way. I guess we'd have to ask them. I'm curious as to what they would say. My guess is that either they wouldn't think of themselves that way or maybe they really don't realize it; they're in denial, they're lying, or they just really don't care. As Hawkeye Pierce once said in an episode of *M*A*S*H*, "How do we manufacture such people?" I wish I had the answer to that one. Maybe each of us needs to model being nice and being kind more often. Imagine if everyone was nice and kind. How nice would that be?

From a speech to students:
On Being Nice and Kind

We all need to care about each other. We need to look after one another. We need to be nice and kind to each other. We need to watch out for each other. After all, that's what it's all about. It's about caring. It's about building relationships. It's about making connections. As human beings, we all need that. We need to feel accepted, we need to feel appreciated, and we need to be paid attention to. Each and every one of us needs to feel connected to other people. None of us are islands unto ourselves. As I've said before, we depend on each other, we rely on each other, and we count on each other. We support each other. We assist each other. We encourage each other. We put our trust in each other and, again, we look after and watch out for each other.

We should also be nice and kind to each other. How easy is it to be nice and kind? How much does it take to be nice and treat each other with respect and love and caring? How do we do that? We do that by being pleasant, by being polite, by being considerate, by being friendly, by being civil, by being nice to all people; by being respectful and caring about other people. We greet each other, we smile at one another, we ask each other how things are going, and we show concern and care for one another. We take care of our family and friends, and we take care of each other. We show and demonstrate being nice and kind. Being nice and kind does not mean that relationships are always perfect. It, however, does mean treating each other respectfully and having a genuine concern and a genuine interest in the well being of another person or persons.

Quite honestly, not many things bother me. However, there are two things that really do bother me: One is when people are not nice and kind and don't care about the feelings or the welfare of other people. People who have no regard for others, for the safety of others, for the health of others, for the feelings of others, or for the well being of others. People who are so selfish that all they think about are themselves. People who are rude, inconsiderate, unfriendly, selfish, unpleasant, and downright mean. They're unpleasant to be around. They're genuinely not nice people. I don't get it. It takes so little to be nice. Truly, you really have to work harder to not be nice. I often wonder if these people wake up every day and say to themselves, "Let's see, how can I not be nice today?" I don't understand that behavior.

Two, what bothers me are people who think they are better than everybody and anybody else. I taught my own daughters the following statement: "Nobody is better than you, and you're no better than anyone else." Be nice and kind to people. It takes so little and means so much.

FROM A SPEECH TO STUDENTS:
ON HOW WE CHOOSE TO TREAT OTHERS

Every day we all have a choice in how we act and behave and how we treat others. I said, and I quote from last month, "We choose to treat people considerately and respectfully and include them, or we choose to ignore them, treat them inappropriately, and exclude them." That statement keeps coming back to me as I think how we often act and behave in our relationships with other people. One of the things that personally makes me most angry and upset is when I see people treating other people disrespectfully, unfairly, inappropriately, and/or just being downright cruel and mean to them. I believe that is so wrong.

We should never purposely embarrass, humiliate, hurt in any way, or make fun of another person for any reason. We should never make fun of others or pick on others. We certainly should never make fun of people because of their race, their religion, their ethnic background, their sexual orientation, their gender, or their socio-economic status – meaning the amount of money and wealth they have or don't have. And we shouldn't make fun of people based on their intellectual abilities; remember that everybody is smart in their own way. You have heard me say, "Nobody is good at everything but everybody is good at something," and we don't make fun of people based on their physical appearance. There are short people and tall people, heavy people and thin people, big and small people.

We don't make fun of people as individuals, and we don't make fun of people as a group. In other words, we don't gang up on people. We don't intimidate people, harrass other people, pick on other people, or as I said before, bully other people. That is not acceptable behavior in any way, shape, or form. We don't harm people through our words or actions. There is no place in a school for it, nor is there a place in the community or in society as a whole for it. If you don't like someone, at least leave him or her alone.

Everyone has a right to like or not like someone, but we do not have a right to make fun of another person or pick on another person. No one has the right to diminish another human being. Everyone has the right to be himself or herself and to be left alone. I personally find picking on people or bullying repulsive and reprehensible. Always remember that "no one is better than you and you are no better than anyone else." When we make fun of or bully other people, we're really just showing our own insecurities and shortcomings and a lack of confidence in ourselves. Making others look bad or bullying or harrassing others does not make us look good. In fact it makes us look foolish. I have no tolerance for people who treat other people inappropriately, disrespectfully, or meanly. It's not nice, it's not right, and it's certainly not funny. No one has the right to bully others, and no one has to be on the receiving end of it and feel that they have no recourse or options. We all come to school to learn and not to be harrassed, intimidated, picked on, or made fun of.

FROM A SPEECH TO STUDENTS:
ON HOW WE CHOOSE TO ACT AND BEHAVE
ON A DAILY BASIS

First of all, I want to wish everyone happy holidays, and a Happy New Year. This is the time of year when we extend good will to everyone. It's a time when all of us are caring and giving. It is a time for us to spread love and cheer to all. I think that's great. Here's my question: Why don't we act and behave that way all year round? All of the time? Why do we have to wait till this time of year to act this way and behave this way? Again, why not always? Here's my challenge: I encourage all of us to think about how we treat each other all of the time.

How much do we give to others during the year? I'm not only talking about gifts, but, more importantly, of ourselves? How do we treat our family and loved ones all year round? How do we treat our colleagues, co-workers, teachers, and students all year round? How do we treat our friends and others all year round? As the new year approaches, many of us will be making resolutions. I suggest that some of those resolutions deal with how we treat other people on a daily basis. I suggest that we all make a conscientious effort to be considerate of others, courteous to others, polite to others, understanding of others, compassionate to others, and empathetic to others. What we say to each other and how we say it is so very important.

Today that feeling we all hopefully have of joy and happiness should be one that we carry around with us all of the time. Our feelings are contagious. Our actions and attitudes and behaviors are contagious. If we make others feel good, we feel good ourselves – and the opposite is also true. If we feel good ourselves, we make others feel good. If we treat someone inappropriately or poorly, we give license for others to do the same. If we show disrespect to someone, we not only hurt that person's feelings, but it also says a lot about who we are as a person. It also tells others that it's okay to treat that person with disrespect. No person deserves to be disrespected, adult or student.

I don't care who you are, I don't care what race you are, what religion you are, what your ethnic background is, whether you're a male or female, what your sexual orientation is, and I don't care how much money you have or don't have. All of those things make absolutely no difference to me on how you should be treated.

Remember that your words and actions to others are so powerful. They are hurtful if they are negative. They are words of inspiration and encouragement, dare I say love and caring, if they are positive. We always need to remember the impact of what we say, how we say it, the words we choose, and the language we use, and what we do – how important our actions, our attitude, and our behaviors are. And we always need to treat everyone respectfully and fairly.

Our school is a place where every student and every teacher should be respected and valued. It is up to ev-

eryone who is a part of this school, the administration, the staff, the parents and the community, and you, the students, to help create that atmosphere. We all do that by not only respecting ourselves but also by respecting others and treating others well. So the language you use, the behaviors we exhibit are all part of that equation.

We should never use language that is inappropriate, demeaning, degrading or hurtful to others or that shows any traces of disrespect against anyone, any individual, any group, anywhere. Not only during this time of giving and sharing should we behave this way, we should behave this way at all times. It should become part of who we are as human beings. How well we treat and respect others is what our school is about, not only this time of year but also all of the time.

FROM A SPEECH TO STUDENTS:
ON BEING NICE AND KIND (AGAIN)

Spring is right around the corner. AH, Spring time. It's time for softball, baseball, lacrosse, tennis, and outdoor track. What a great time of year. When it's nice, warm, and sunny out, it seems as if people are even more pleasant and nicer. Or so they appear to be. Maybe even kinder, as well. Many people have smiles on their faces when spring comes around. I know I do. It would be nice if that were the case all year round. Quite frankly, I sometimes get cranky when it's cold and dark outside.

As I was thinking about what to write about and talk about today, I looked over the words that I always end with and wanted to focus on the part that says: "Care about and take care of each other, look out and watch out for each other, and be nice and kind to each other." And I said to myself, do we really do that all of the time? Do we care about and take care of each other? Do we really look out and watch out for one another? Are we nice and kind to each other? I'm sure we are – sometimes. I'm not sure we are all of the time. Nevertheless, I believe that those behaviors and actions are and should be a part of who we are as people on a daily basis. It should be part of our being. Sometimes we are so immersed in our own lives, in our own issues, our own challenges and problems, that we forget about others and their issues, their challenges, and their problems. We become so self-centered and self-absorbed that everything revolves around us. And I'm not saying that we should not pay attention to ourselves, we certainly need to take care of ourselves and solve our problems, but that is no excuse not to be kind and nice, pleasant and considerate, well-mannered and respectable, and civil to others at all times. We should always be showing concern and understanding for others, being compassionate and empathetic toward others, dare I say, being nice and kind. There is really no excuse not to be nice to someone.

The biggest compliment I have ever gotten is when someone says to me, "You've got nice kids." There's nothing that can top that. Being nice means being pleasant, considerate, caring, well mannered, civil, and respectable to others, including our family, our friends, our fellow classmates, and people we just happen to meet. Being kind means showing sympathy and empathy when needed, concern and understanding for others. Nice and kind are also verbal and non-verbal actions. It's not just about what we say; it's about how we say it. It's also about what we do, our actions and behaviors. It's about our facial expressions, our body language, and our communication in all aspects of our personality. Rolling our eyes at someone or making a face at someone is not nice. Making fun of someone or others is not nice. Not helping others when they need our help and support is not nice. If you really want to know if someone is nice and kind, watch how they treat their parents, their siblings, their friends, and/or other people they may come across or meet. Also, watch how they act when things don't go their way, or when they don't get what they want! We can all be nice and kind when things are going well and we get what we want. How about when we don't? How do we act then?

Some of the most important qualities one possesses are to be nice and to be kind. To be considerate of others. To care about others, take care of others, watch out for others, look out for others, just as you would like others to care about you, watch out for you, take care of you, and look out for you. One of the ugliest words in the English language is the word, "mean." No one likes a mean person. I don't even like the sound of the word, it makes me shudder. Mean is the opposite of nice. It's being evil. There is no place for mean. I believe that people that are mean and mean to other people really don't like who they are; they don't like themselves so they try to make other people look bad by being mean to them so they can look good. It doesn't work that way. Never has. Never will. So always try to be nice and kind.

15
The Importance of Self-Control

I know that the word control can have both a positive and negative connotation. What I mean by control here is only in its most positive form, specifically self-control. I believe that people should always be in control of their behavior, their attitude, and their actions. We must have the power and ability to manage ourselves at all times. It also does not negate asking for help if we need it. In fact, I encourage it. It does not negate seeking guidance, assistance, support, or varying opinions and viewpoints.

What I am saying is that we must always be able to control our actions, logically manage ourselves in all situations, not lose control of our behaviors, and not be so easily influenced by the actions of others in a negative way. When we are easily led or easily influenced, when we give in to peer pressure or give in when we know in our hearts and minds that we're right, then we are giving up our control of ourselves. We must never let another individual or individuals influence us negatively. We must never let another individual or group of people control us to the point that we are not thinking for ourselves.

In addition, we should never give up control of ourselves to substances that "make" us behave in a way that, under normal conditions, we would never behave. Control is a significant concept that should be used in the most positive way. People like to be in control, but they first need to be in control of themselves. (This in no way implies that people who like control should be able to control others). Again, all people should think for themselves and rely on other people for support, help, assistance, encouragement, and inspiration, and not let themselves be controlled by other people. That's a no-no.

FROM A SPEECH TO STUDENTS:
ON BEING IN CONTROL OF OURSELVES

We need to take control of our lives and be responsible for our own actions. Too frequently we take things, including life itself, for granted and we forget. Remember, we can never go back and undo or redo what is already done. We can say we're sorry, we can try and change some things, but there are some things that once they are done are done forever and can never, ever be changed. So, when we're making our choices and decisions, we need to always remember that. Our choices and decisions may have an impact on us and others for the rest of our lives.

I want to always know exactly what I am doing. Call it control because I always do want to be in control of myself. With regards to peer pressure, never, ever, let another person or group of people dictate to you what to do or influence your actions, especially if in your heart, if in your gut, you know it's not the right thing. And, don't ever let a substance take over your thought process. You don't impress people by caving in; then they are in control. You impress people, but more than that, you impress yourself when you make the decisions and you're in control. We all have the ability to make our own decisions and choices and not be influenced by the negative peer pressures of others.

Regarding the use of substances: Don't ever let a substance take over your thought process. Personally, I don't use substances. Never have. Never will. And I

certainly don't like having substances control someone's behavior. To young people: Use of substances
is illegal. Understand that. Being under the control of
substances is dangerous and can be, and unfortunately
is, the cause of much harm, injury, and even death. To
older people: The very same holds true. I don't mean to
preach to you, but please be aware of the consequences
of your behavior and actions if you're under the influence of substances. You no longer have control. The
substances do!

16
The Importance of
Hope and Optimism

Hope springs eternal. We all want to believe in a bright future. We want that for ourselves and we want that for our children. We want to trust that the future holds good things for everyone. We expect and anticipate the best. We hope for it and we look forward to it.

We really live in three worlds – the past, which is over, the present, which is brief (life is as it is at that moment), and the future, which is ahead of us and truly unknown. Most of us did things in the past and do things in the present in preparation for that unknown future. But hope always remains. And hope should remain – for if and when we lose hope, our life can become unhappy and depressing because we feel that we have nothing to look forward to. Hope is the solution to that. And along with hope comes optimism – the hope and the confidence and the attitude that the future will, in fact, be bright and that things will always turn out okay.

To be optimistic is, in my mind, not to be foolish or simplistic, but rather to be hopeful and confident, though not unrealistic. Realism has to be, I believe, part of optimism. Martin Seligman from the University of Pennsylvania says in his research that optimistic people are generally happier, healthier, live longer, and are more successful than their counterparts, the pessimists.

FROM A SPEECH TO STUDENTS:
ON MOTIVATION AND OPPORTUNITY

I began to think of two concepts, both of which have a place in all of our lives – the concepts of motivation and opportunity. I asked myself: What really motivates people to do things, to do well or not do well, to succeed, to keep going even when the odds seem to be against them, or when they have faced frustration, defeat, and disappointment? And, why don't more people take advantage of all of the opportunities available in this school, in this county, in this country, in this world, to do better, to make something of themselves, to succeed in whatever they're good at and interested in? Why do some people seem to be able to keep going while others seem to give up? The answers did not come quickly or easily. I continued to ponder this issue. I believe that motivation comes from within.

It's about desire, determination, and perseverance. It's about having goals and having dreams and being optimistic and hopeful about one's future. It's about having confidence in ourselves and our abilities, whatever they may be. Remember, we all have abilities, each and every one of us, though they are different for each person. It's about the desire to continue to improve ourselves, it's about working with others and helping others to achieve their goals. It is about understanding that life is going to have some ups and downs, and it is those of us that can handle these often unexpected bumps in the road or detours who can bounce back and continue on track.

Motivation to do well in whatever we choose to do, with that positive attitude that I spoke to you about previously, are the two keys to our success and happiness. And isn't that what we all want? Who doesn't want to be happy and successful in life? I never met anyone who didn't want it, though I've met several people who didn't quite know how to achieve it. Without either, motivation or opportunity, we drift through life with no direction. And just think of all the opportunities there are. The freedoms we enjoy to explore what we like, to take calculated risks, to try new and different things, to learn from each other, to interact with each other, to meet people who are experts in their areas and who would want nothing more than to pass on their knowledge, skills, and wisdom to us, which we will then hopefully pass on to others. That to me is exciting. And what better time than the beginning of the school year where we all have a fresh start, regardless of the past, to take advantage of the knowledge, skills, and wisdom of our teachers, our parents, our coaches or advisors, our counselors, and other adults who are significant in our lives. What a time to meet new people, new teachers, new classmates. And don't forget our current friends who also possess certain knowledge and skills and who are also part of our support system. Friends should always help us and be there for us and give us good, honest advice.

What a great time to really get off to a great start. If you've done well in the past, continue along. You have created the habits and attitudes that will take you successfully through life. If the past has not been as successful as you would like, the time is now to get started. The opportunity is here for you. It always is. It's just the later you wait the more difficult it gets. The motivation to do well and succeed has to and can start right now. Go for it. Everyone around you is willing to pitch in and help. All you've got to do is ask and take some action yourself. If everything in life was easy, then everybody could do it. We need to take control of our lives, we need to help ourselves, take positive action and positive steps, and we will be amazed at the amount of people that will help us, assist us, and support us.

The time to begin and/or continue is now. I wish you all good luck, but more than that I urge everyone to develop that inner motivation to do well and take advantage of the opportunities available to all of you. Staff, I implore you to continuously motivate and inspire your students. Students, you need to motivate yourselves. Motivation of others is great, but the best motivation comes from within.

FROM A SPEECH TO STUDENTS:
ON OPTIMISM

Over the years, one of the concepts I've become interested in is the concept of optimism and its relationship to success. Both optimism and pessimism are attitudes, mindsets, lifestyles.

Optimism is defined as a tendency to expect the best possible outcome or to dwell upon the most hopeful aspects of a situation. Optimists believe the world is more good than evil. This is in contrast to pessimism, which is defined as a tendency to take the gloomiest possible view of a situation and the belief that the evil in the world outweighs the good. Optimists statistically tend to be healthier, happier, live longer, be less stressed, and be more successful than their counterparts, the pessimists. Optimists do not let failures, or as I've always called them, "temporary setbacks," stop them from their pursuit of their goals. In fact, optimists, when faced with setbacks, disappointments or "failures," become even more determined and eventually overcome the setbacks, which then spurs them even more so on to victory or success. Optimists persevere and do not let anything stand in their way toward their accomplishments and achievements. Optimists are determined to succeed. They look for what's right and good.

Pessimists, on the other hand, tend to give up after a defeat, loss, failure, rejection, disappointment, or setback and have difficulty re-establishing themselves and getting back on track. Pessimistic people look at every-

thing, including the world itself, in a negative way. They never have hope that things will change or get better or that they have some control over what happens to them. They tend to blame others and not take responsibility. They accept defeat as another reason that life is so miserable.

Optimists, on the other hand, look at everything, including the world in general, in a positive manner. They never lose hope that things will get better and that they have the ability within themselves to change things. They believe that they have some control over their path in life. Optimists look at defeat or setbacks as a challenge to try harder. It makes them more determined. Optimists never give up.

Having said all of this, the other part of the equation is our sense of reality. I mean that even when we're optimistic we have to have a realistic sense of what is happening and what is possible. In other words, I'm an optimistic person but I understand that there are some limitations to my abilities in certain areas. So, I choose those areas of my strength and those areas I have a passion for, and I work to be successful in those areas. I'm optimistic that I can be successful in those areas. I fully understand what I am capable of and what I am not capapble of. Yet, I still work hard to be the best I can be in those areas where I don't excel. That's being optimistic, but it's also being realistic.

We will all face some challenges in life. And, in whatever we do, we need to do it well, do it the best we can, and never lose that optimism about life in general.

We must continue to be optimistic about our own path within life. We also always have to be ready to change, to adapt, and to face the new challenges that face us every day. Optimism will help us successfully deal with those changes and challenges.

We all know the people who are always complaining that nothing is right. My advice to them: Stop the complaining and do something constructive and productive to make it right. Nothing changes by complaining and doing nothing. Things change for the better when the complaining stops and we take positive, constructive, and productive action; when we adapt. That's another difference between a pessimist and an optimist. A pessimist will complain and do nothing. An optimist, if they have a concern, will do something about it. They will take that positive action. Optimists don't use the excuse that they don't have the power to do something or they're not in a position to do something. They believe, and I agree with them, that everyone has the power to do something if they want to. Saying you don't is just an excuse. It takes optimists and people of conviction to get things done. Optimists take responsibility and they don't blame others for their life's situation.

Given the choice, why wouldn't we all want to be optimists? Well, that's where we and our attitudes come in. If we see ourselves as pessimists, we need to change our attitudes and become more positive. Remember the quote: "It doesn't matter where you've been. It only matters where you're going"? Optimists plan for the future. Optimists have a vision for the future. Optimists are hopeful. Pessimists look for excuses. Optimists look for opportunities. Optimists wake up every morning looking at the challenge of accomplishing something useful and productive every day and look at challenges as an opportunity to succeed. In order to be successful, we've got to believe that we can be successful. It's our choice. I know which one I would choose. I hope you will, too.

FROM A SPEECH TO STUDENTS:

ON HOPE

Today I want to discuss the concept of hope. No matter how difficult things can be at times, no matter how stressful life can often appear, hope is always there.

The dictionary defines hope as something that is desired or having an expectation for something. That definition didn't quite do it for me, so I came up with my own definition and the context in which I think of hope. In other words, what it means to me. I believe that hope is a feeling, a belief, an optimistic feeling and belief and a desire that things in life can be and will be better. It is always believing, in our minds and in our hearts, that we can rise above the issues, the problems, the challenges, and the conflicts that sometimes befall all of us during our lifetime. It is believing that we can work to comprehend and understand the issues and to then find solutions and resolutions for them. And that means not giving up and keeping the hope, the feeling, the belief, and the desire alive.

We all know in life there will be challenges, there will be problems and issues to deal with, and it is our ability to deal with them that will get us through. An important part of hope is not only our own thinking and feelings and not giving up, it is also knowing that there is support for us, help for us, guidance for us, from many places and many people, including right here in this building. Hope is knowing that we are not ever hanging out there on our own. We are not alone. I don't want any of us to ever give up hope, to ever feel that no one cares. That's part of what we do as educators, and I would emphatically say that there is no adult in this building that does not care about every student in this building.

As some of us move on from here, there will be others who will care, and there will always be us who will always care. Never hesitate to share with us or with each other what is going on. As adults, we cannot read your minds. We need to communicate with each other. You need to communicate with us and we need to communicate with you, and we will provide the support you need or at least refer you to the people who are better equipped to provide that support.

Life has its ups and down. It has its peaks and valleys. It has, as we say, its good days and its bad days. What we will always need to remember is that we need to believe, again, in our minds and in our hearts, that we have the power and the control to make things better, to make a difference, to help ourselves and others, especially in times of need and to never, ever give up on ourselves or others in the most difficult and challenging situations. That is hope. And we are never alone; even at times if we think we are.

I believe in my heart that the love and support we give to each other helps each one of us when things are not going as well as we would like. That's what life is. And whatever any of us is dealing with, there is always hope, there is always help, there is alway support. It is often looking in the right places. I pledge to you my *own personal support to anyone listening if you should ever need it. I may not always have the answer or the solution, but I will always try to find the answer or help you find the solution or refer you to someone who can assist you and help you. And I believe that I am not the only one who will make that commitment to you. We all have many people out there, family and friends, people who care about us and would be very willing to assist you, me, and everyone else who needs it. I will leave you with this final thought regarding hope: Hope is what keeps us going. Hope is what keeps us thriving. As long as we are alive, there is always hope, for hope springs eternal.*

Endnote: The student who spoke to me about hope and asked me to talk about hope and who inspired this piece was a blind young lady. She has never given up hope. I dedicate this passage to her for inspiring me with her own courage and determination to hold on to hope and optimism, despite the challenges she faced growing up.

17

The Importance of
Compassion and Empathy

I f you ever get a chance, I highly recommend that you read
Daniel Goleman's book, *Emotional Intelligence*. Dr. Goleman talks extensively about compassion and empathy in his
book. It will give you a great perspective on what's really important to be successful.

Compassion is having sympathy for the suffering of others,
often including a desire to help. Empathy is the ability to identi-
fy and understand another person's feelings and/or difficulties. I
can't think of two better human traits than compassion and empathy. Compassionate and empathetic people are truly exceptional
individuals. I truly believe that two of the major character traits
that separate people from one another are the qualities of compassion and empathy. Their caring and concern for others is un-
paralleled. I truly believe that people who have compassion and
empathy really make a difference in other people's lives. These
people are our support people, our "go to" people, and our rock.
I believe that these two traits are essential for successful relationships among people both in their personal and professional lives.

From a speech to students:
On Compassion and Empathy

Today I'd like to discuss with you two terms that I think are as important in our interactions with each other as any two terms could be. They are compassion and empathy. Compassion is our ability to sympathize with others and have a desire to help and assist in any way we can. Empathy is our ability to truly understand another person's feelings by "being in their shoes."

Life has many challenges, and as I've told you several times before, it is often our ability to successfully deal with these challenges and "bounce back" from unexpected events that may happen in our life that allows us to successfully move on. While we are in the midst of these challenges, it helps greatly if there are people who are there to help us, support us, and assist us – people who demonstrate compassion and show empathy. How fortunate we are when we have people who show that compassion and empathy. It is frequently that compassion and empathy that gives us that extra boost to deal with our challenges.

It takes a special person to be compassionate and empathetic. It takes effort and a strong desire to truly and sincerely "feel" for other people and be able and willing to assist them and support them. I will tell you that the pay off for those individuals that you do that for is truly appreciated and cherished. I encourage all of you to develop the skills of compassion and empathy. They are two traits that you will never regret hav-

ing, and they will make a great deal of difference in your life and in the lives of others.

18
The Importance of
Humor and Laughter
(and a Smile)

I always say in my concluding remarks to students, "Maintain your sense of humor; you'll always need that." How true I believe that is. Humor and laughter are truly the best medicines. How important is it to laugh? How important is it to see humor in some things? Very, very important.

I specifically say "some" things because there are things that are not funny and not humorous. Each person has to be his or her own judge of that. I believe, however, that we should never make fun of something or someone when another individual or group of people is taking something very seriously and does not think it is funny. As I've always said, laugh with people, not at people.

Going along with humor and laughter is the always-welcome smile. People like people who smile. A smile generally lightens things up a bit, if not a lot.

Laughter and a smile are both universal languages. Everyone recognizes and understands them. Again, however, timing is everything. In other words, know where and when it is appropriate to laugh and be festive. In most situations it is very appropriate. In others, it may not be.

FROM A SPEECH TO STUDENTS:
ON SMILING

A couple of weeks ago, I was on the phone with a good friend of mine, Alan, whom I know from kindergarten. Let me tell you that kindergarten for me is a long time ago. If any of you students know anyone going back to kindergarten that you're still friendly with, that's going back anywhere from 10 to 13 years, depending on what grade you're in. Since I just turned 58 years old in December, my friendship with Alan goes back 53 years. How about that? That is a long time, and it also says something about our friendship. (That friendship also shaped my life; it was through Alan and his younger sister, Lynn, that I met my wife Rita because Lynn was, and still is, friendly with Rita, and I was friendly with Alan. We met when I was 19 and she was 17. We will be married 35 years in February. You just never know, do you?)

Anyway, in our conversation a few weeks ago, Alan and I were reminiscing about our childhood and ball-playing days back in New York City. We played ball together all the way through high school and then played against each other in college. Admittedly, he was a much better ballplayer than I was. As we spoke and laughed, and talked about our escapades and some of the people we hung out with and played ball with, we both quickly realized how much time had elapsed. We said to each other: Where did the time go? How quickly it passed by. We're both in our 50's now! How did that happen? We're not 17 years old anymore? No we're not, and we can't do what we used to – at least as well. We both laughed. As we ended the conversation and were about to hang up, he said to me a couple of words that will stay with me forever: "Larry," he said, "take care of yourself, stay healthy and keep smiling." Wow. I was struck. I was inspired. The "Take care of yourself and stay healthy" part is what I often say and, of course, I feel is included and implied in my "Come back to us safely on Monday" statement. But the "keep smiling" part really struck a chord and touched a nerve. I said to myself, "That's it. I need to include that in my talks. I need to talk about that. I need to emphasize that." I was excited and energized by it.

You see, at 58 I'm still learning also. So here it is. I always say to you in my ending remarks, "Maintain your sense of humor; you'll always need that," and I truly believe that. I strongly believe in having a sense of humor. I also always say, "Smile often; laugh with others, not at others," and I believe that as well. But, "keep smiling," really said it all. There is nothing like a smile that says hello to people, that welcomes people, that evokes happiness, makes people feel good, makes people feel safe and comfortable, makes you feel good. It makes all of us feel good. A smile is universal language. It's contagious. It says it all. It says, "It's nice to see you," "I'm happy and glad to see you," "I'm happy, and I hope you're happy," "It's good to be alive," among many other things. A smile is a sign of happiness, a sign of acceptance, a sign of love, a sign of peace, a sign of joy and contentment. A smile brings people together. A smile creates an atmosphere of warmth, caring, hope, and optimism. I honestly can't think of anything nicer than a smile.

So, here's my challenge and here's my hope for everyone listening – adults and students alike: My challenge for you is to smile as often as you can, to form the habit of smiling, to make it a part of your being. Sometimes, you got to smile even when you really don't feel like smiling. It will make you feel better. My hope is that you always have reason to smile. Even when things are not going quite the way you want them, I hope that you can find a reason to smile. I hope that whatever challenges and stresses you may have in life or you may face, that a smile by you to others and by others to you will make your life and other people's lives a little more (if not a lot more) pleasant, enjoyable, and happy. A smile may just make your day. Like everything else, smiling is a choice. It always comes back to choice. So, my choice – and I hope your choice – is to keep smiling.

FROM A SPEECH TO STUDENTS:
ON LAUGHING

My announcement this morning will be brief. About a month ago a friend of both my wife and myself, Elaine, called the house and said that she had had a tough day at work that day. I know we've all had those. Then she said, "Larry, do me a favor, make me laugh." I admit that nothing is better than a good laugh, and I was both taken back a bit and also flattered. I was taken back because how was I going to make someone laugh on the spot. That's pressure. I was flattered that she thought I could do it because I like to laugh and I like when other people are laughing. I really like when people make me laugh. Well, somehow, I did it. I don't remember what I said or did and we all laughed. Here's my point: We do need to make each other laugh, especially when someone else needs it. Laughter is great medicine for a tough day, a bad mood, or an uncomfortable situation, but having said that, the timing must be right and the person must want to laugh. You can't, and shouldn't, make someone laugh when they are not ready because then you risk not taking them or their situation seriously when they are in distress or in need of support.

So, use laughter appropriately and carefully and under the right circumstances. It can be and often is the best medicine, and it can and often does break the tension. I love to laugh, I love to make people laugh, and, most of all, I love when others make me laugh. So here's a challenge for all of you: Make me laugh!

19

The Importance of
Trust

Nothing cements a relationship like trust. Nothing destroys a relationship like mistrust. It is probably the most important factor in any relationship, along with mutual respect. And nothing takes longer to build up and a split second to destroy. When you trust, you believe in that person totally and completely, you have 100% faith in their character and integrity, you have the utmost confidence in their being.

All successful relationships are built on trust. Without trust there can be no true, lasting relationship.

Trust takes a long time to build and just a moment to destroy. I have seen far too many relationships, both personally and professionally, come apart because trust was broken and destroyed. Trust is built by both our words and our actions as well as our attitude and choices. When we have gained someone's trust, we have received the highest honor. When we have bestowed our trust upon someone else, we have given that person our highest honor. Please do not take trust lightly. It is quite a responsibility on all of us, but one we should seek and cherish.

FROM A SPEECH TO STUDENTS:
ON TRUST

I was thinking the other day about the word trust. I began to focus on people in my own life whom I trust implicitly. That means that I trust them totally and completely. I have the utmost confidence in their character and integrity; I believe that they would do anything for me, as I would do anything for them, of course always within the rule of law and morality.

The people I trust most are my family: my wife, my children, my siblings, and my parents when they were alive. I believe that none of these people would ever let me down as I would never let them down as well. There are also my friends: people whom I have known for years that are almost like family. I don't think that any of my family or friends has ever violated my trust and confidence. The reality is that it takes just one time to violate a trust and then, quite honestly, it is very difficult to trust that particular person ever again.

Students, it is important that you trust that we as adults have your best interests at heart. It is also important that adults in this building also maintain that professional trust and always act in the best interests of the students. Trust is the cornerstone of any successful relationship, be it in the family, in the school, in the workplace, or within your social circle.

Trust is essential if a relationship is to progress and endure. I encourage everyone to be trustworthy and to understand the importance of this all-important word.

Trust is a two-way street. Trust of others is not something we automatically give another person or persons. They must earn it as we must earn theirs.

20

The Importance of
Passion and a Sense of Purpose

L ife has a purpose. People who believe that they have a purpose and can shape a vision for themselves are generally happier and more successful. They also make a difference in the world. That vision, that purpose, that passion is different for everyone. As I've stated many times before, we all possess certain skills and talents. We also have many different interests. If we can take those skills, talents, and interests and develop them into something we love to do, we are on our way to implementing that vision and passion.

Our work, our involvement in activities, including voluntary activities, often is a result of our passion and our desire to have a sense of purpose and leave a legacy after we are gone. Passion is that excitement, energy, and enthusiasm that gives life its meaning. A purpose gives us a reason to live.

I believe that everyone should have a purpose in life. I believe that everyone should have goals to achieve and things to accomplish. That's part of what makes life fun and challenging. We're all only going to spend a certain, unspecified amount of time on this Earth, and I encourage all of us to create a vision, find a passion, seek a purpose, follow our dreams, and work hard to accomplish our mission. There is ample opportunity for all of us to be successful if we choose to do so. The worst thing would be to get to the end of our life and say, "I wish I had. . .," "I should have. . .," or "I could have. . . ."

FROM A SPEECH TO STUDENTS:
ON HARD WORK, PASSION, AND A SENSE OF PURPOSE

I believe that an essential key to our success in the present and in the future – where we are going to live the rest of our lives – is our determination to succeed in whatever tasks or endeavors we attempt. Our passion and our sense of purpose drives us. Success in following our passion does not come without sacrifice. Our ability not to give up and our ability to work hard directly contributes to our successes. Hard work is one of the main ingredients and keys to success in anything we do. With that passion and sense of purpose, followed by the hard work, we can achieve our goals. Raw talent only carries us so far. Hard work and passion and a sense of purpose takes us to the next level, to the top, to excellence.

This same concept pertains to your classes. Grades are not given. Grades are earned, and grades are earned by not only your ability to comprehend and understand the material, but by the hard work and passion that you put into it. Someone once said, "If everything was easy, anyone could do it." And, like I've said many times before, "not everyone can do everything, but everybody can do something"; in order to do that "something" really well, it takes having a sense of purpose, passion, and hard work.

If all success were attributed to luck, then we'd all

just sit around, wait, and hope for good luck to happen. We can't afford to do that. Having passion and a sense of purpose and hard work has gotten all of us to where we are today. And, hard work is not a negative. In fact, it's positive and can be fun because there is nothing like the sense of satisfaction and accomplishment and the feeling of joy in our success after we have put a great deal of hard work into something. Don't you feel good after you've put hard work, time, and effort into something and it works out? There is no substitute for hard work and for the satisfaction of what it accomplishes. There is no substitute for passion. The challenge of it all and the successful completion of our attempts make it all worthwhile in the end. And if it doesn't work out at first, then we go back and try again. That determination to not give up and to try and try again eventually leads to success. We can't let the passion die.

Hard work is an attitude and habit. Hard work never hurt anybody, but lack of hard work and lack of determination, and a lack of passion and a lack of a sense of purpose, has hurt many people who have had the potential, the ability, and the talent to be successful but refused to spend their time wisely, and to work hard to bring that talent, that gift, that ability to their fullest potential. Being passionate and working hard and not doing as well as you might like is not the problem; it's not trying at all or giving up that is the problem. Let me conclude by giving you a personal example.

When I speak with you every Friday, I want you to know that I work hard on these talks. It takes me time to do this. This is not a one-time shot because I take it *very seriously* and I work hard on it. In fact, I start *days* ahead; I jot down notes and ideas that I think of and that others give me. I write different drafts before it comes to you on Friday. In fact, today's talk is actually the fourth or fifth draft that I wrote, and I made the last changes at 6:30 this morning before I left my house.

I encourage all of you, again, to use your time wisely and work hard in whatever you do. Hard work, using time wisely, plus the always-important good, positive attitude will get you where you want to go. It's not going to happen by accident or by luck. It's going to happen because you work hard to make it happen and you are passionate about what you're doing. The question always is: Are you looking to do the best that you can for as long as you can, or are you looking to get away with as much as you can for as long as you can?

Endnote: My passion in writing this book allowed me to complete it and get it published. Nothing was going to stop me. Did I have doubts if I would get it done and get it published? Absolutely. Did that stop me? No. I was determined and passionate about getting it done and my sense of purpose – to help others – drove me to its completion.

21

The Importance of Balance in Our Lives

My father always said, "Everything in moderation. Nothing to the extreme." He was a wise man. I wish he were still here.

Our lives are pulled in many different ways. We wear many different hats. We may be parents, we all were somebody's children and may still be, if our parents are still alive. We may be siblings, friends, workers, students, and we may be involved in a variety of activities. We also have our daily living necessities to take care of – eating, sleeping, and taking care of ourselves mentally, physically, emotionally, socially, psychologically, and spiritually. In addition, we are, for the most part, social beings, and we manage (or are at least we are a part of) a household. We have lots to take care of and much we are responsible for. All that in a daily routine of 24 hours a day. (Just writing this, I'm tired already.) How do we do it all? How do we find the time and energy? Many of us do it day in and day out successfully. Others, unfortunately, continue to struggle and are not as successful in balancing it all out. It does take balancing and prioritizing.

Again, some of us have it easier and it may be that we have less to do and we started out with more resources, while others have it more difficult because they may have more to do and they may have less resources, help, support, and assistance. It is quite the balancing act. My recommendation and suggestion in simple terms, though I understand that it's not that simple at all in the real world: Take time and try and put your life in balance. Get access to the needed resources. Try and get organized and develop a routine. Balance the professional you, the work you, and the home you. Life is always going to be a balance, and we must constantly be aware of the demands and the things we have to do and the things we want to do. It is my hope that we can get both the "have to's and the "want to's" done successfully. Try to get organized the best way you can and for some of us (myself included), I know that this is a challenge. In fact, I'm really still trying to figure that one out myself.

FROM A SPEECH TO STUDENTS:
ON BALANCE IN OUR LIVES

Good morning. I know that sometimes we all feel a bit overwhelmed and stressed with the "Oh, so many things we need to do." I know I feel it and I know you feel it. We all feel it. There is no magic answer, and each one of us deals with it all differently. However, sometimes, quite frankly, we need to step back, take a deep breath, think, and refocus. Sometimes, we even need to reprioritize. As I said when we talked about time, we all have the very same 24 hours a day/7 days a week. And, as students and adults, we all need to work at balancing everything out. For students: You all go to school, you have class work and homework and projects, you may very well participate in extracurricular activities, be that sports, drama, music, or the various school clubs that are available. You may be involved in community activities, you may hold down a job, and you may have household responsibilities. And, of course you have your social life with your friends. As adults, we have jobs. As teachers we plan and prepare lessons, we grade papers, we have professional development, we communicate with parents and colleagues, and we, too, may have families and have family responsibilities and obligations, in addition to our social life with friends. So, you see, it can get overwhelming at times.

Balance in our lives means a couple of things to me. It means, first and foremost, making sure that we get organized and get our priorities in order so we do get the things that need to get done, done, so that we can do the things we want to do and enjoy them. There are "have-to's" and "want to's"; if we get the "have-to's" done, we will enjoy the "want-to's" much more. If not, we'll be thinking about the "have-to's" as we're doing the "want-to's." That makes for stress. Having said all of that, it is extremely important that we all take time to make sure that we give balance to our lives so that we don't get so bogged down with one aspect of our life that we neglect the other parts of it. For example, for students: I always encourage you to work hard and to do your very best in the classroom and in your studies. That is a priority in my mind. However, I also encourage you to have a life outside of the classroom. I encourage participation in extracurricular activities. I encourage your involvement in school or community groups and activities. I encourage you to have a social life, and I encourage you to be involved with your families and friends. To teachers: I encourage you to make sure you spend time with your families and enjoy recreational activities.

Life is many things. It is work and it is play. It is being involved and being active. It is family and it is friends. It is responsibility and it is recreational and social activities. Try to experience the many offerings and opportunities that life has, and always try to balance it all out so that you can do as much as you can successfully and happily. There is a time for everything. Try to balance it all out and enjoy the ride.

22
The Importance of
Health and Safety

N othing is more important to me than our health and safety. I would venture to say that nothing is more important
to a parent than their child's health, safety, and welfare.
It's priority #1, as well it should be. All of my decisions as a parent when my children were young were based on their health and
safety. It still is as they are now young adults.

When you don't have your health and safety, other things pale
in comparison. We also have a tendency to take our health and
safety for granted. Don't!

FROM A SPEECH TO STUDENTS:
ON HEALTH AND SAFETY

Because of the upcoming holidays, we are hopefully all in festive moods, and we may very well be attending parties to celebrate the different holidays including New Years. As always, I encourage you and urge you to act in a safe and responsible manner. I want you to know, if you don't already know, that since the beginning of this school year, 17 young people in the Baltimore/ Washington/Northern Virginia area, all high school students, have lost their lives in traffic accidents. And it's only the beginning of December. All of the accidents have been due to either speeding or drinking and driving or a combination of both. Two of the 17 students were local students at other high schools.

When I think of the term "accident," I think of something that didn't happen or occur on purpose. After all, the definition of "accident" is "an unexpected and undesirable event." So by definition, it happens because "something just happens." So it's called an accident. I was thinking about that and here's my take on it: It certainly is undesirable, but is it really unexpected? I often question that. Something happens because someone or some group of people cause it to happen. It may not have been planned, but by their actions it was certainly within the realm of possibility. What do I mean by that? Well, the only real or true accident in my view is a natural occurrence or natural disaster. Lightning striking someone is an accident. No one person or persons caused it; it was a natural occurrence. An earthquake causing death and destruction is an accident. Damage done by hurricanes or tornadoes similarly are accidents. No one's actions caused them to happen. (Not that I understand why they happen, either. Again, I'm still trying to figure all of that out myself.)

Therefore, to me that means that everything else is not an accident, but an incident, often an unfortunate event, and that someone's actions caused something else to happen. For example, if we do things we shouldn't do, are careless or reckless, something may happen that we consciously didn't expect to happen and is undesirable; it easily could have been avoided had we given it more thought, made wiser choices and decisions, and used better judgment. People driving fast and recklessly, people driving under the influence of alcohol and/or other drugs, people talking on cell phones and/or texting and not paying attention to what they're doing, people tailgating or not stopping for red lights or stop signs, people doing other foolish things that cause the death or injury to themselves or someone else is not really an accident, although I'm certain that they didn't mean to cause a problem. It is, in fact, truly a lack of good judgment and poor choices and poor decisions, and yet it causes pain and suffering to those injured and their families. It's just that our actions may have caused something to happen that we refer to as an accident.

It is within that framework that we must all think about what we're doing and the decisions we're making when it can impact ourselves and/or others, especially in a very negative way. To me, there is nothing more important than our health and safety. Those of you who know me know how I feel about that. We take care of our health by doing the right things – eating right, getting enough rest, exercising, not smoking or using drugs and/or alcohol, generally taking good care of ourselves. We take care of our safety the best way we can by the decisions we make, the choices we make, the judgment we use. Hence, as I always say in ending my talks, make good choices and good decisions, use good judgment, and come back to us safely on Monday.

From a speech to students:
On Being Smart With Our Choices
and Decisions

Good morning. I'd like to talk with you today about being smart with our choices and decisions. Please be smart. Use good common sense. Be intelligent with your decisions, make good choices, and use good judgment. Please don't do foolish things that may hurt, harm, injure, and, in the worst-case scenario, kill someone or yourself. Being smart is not speeding, not driving fast and recklessly, and not trying to show off. That kind of stuff is not smart, and it's certainly not cool. In fact, it's foolish.

Smart is not being on the cell phone and/or texting while you're driving. Smart is paying attention to the road at all times and focusing on what you're doing, which is driving. Remember, you are not only responsible for yourself in the car; you are also responsible for your passengers and the other people on the road as well. At least do your part because, unfortunately, you can't control other people's behavior. You can only hope that they're as smart as you in this. Smart is also not drinking and/or doing other drugs. That's foolish. Really foolish is drinking and/or doing other drugs and driving. That's beyond foolish – that's unacceptable and stupid (pardon the term, but it is)! Again, please use good judgment and make good decisions. Please always be in control of your actions and behaviors. And, here's the last thing – when you see a friend or an acquain-

tance doing something foolish, let them know and try to stop them the best way you can, because if you don't say anything or do anything, then that's really telling them that what they're doing is okay, and it's not. And, if they don't listen, you at least be smart and stay away from them yourself and help keep others away. If that ruins a friendship, so be it. It's certainly better than ruining a life. I have seen many so-called "smart and otherwise intelligent people" do some really dumb, stupid, and foolish things. Don't be one of those people. Don't be a statistic. I often wonder, what were they thinking? If in your heart and gut you feel something is wrong or feels wrong, it probably is. Please let this be a lifelong lesson because even some adults, on occasion, have done some very foolish things.

Please do not misunderstand me. I'm not saying don't have fun. Quite the contrary. Very few people have more fun in life than I do. Just ask my family and friends. But I am never out of control of my behavior and actions and have never been. Those who know me know that I never drink or have never used other substances. So certainly, have fun. Enjoy yourself. Have a good time. What I am saying, though, is be smart. Have good, clean fun. Not foolish fun. Have fun with people, not at the expense of people. Don't do anything to jeopardize the safety of anyone, including yourself. Never lose control of what you're doing. Yes, laugh lots. Have a good time. But, again, be smart. What I don't want for you is to be out of control and I don't want your mistakes, your misjudgment to lead to disaster and tragedy.

From a speech to students:
On Survival and Invincibility

Today I have two words I'd like to discuss with you: Survival and Invincibility. Why these two words? Well, a couple of reasons. Within the last two months or so, another two local car accidents have occurred. One involved a graduating senior from last year who suffered very serious injuries and another involved some other seniors this year, one of whom was killed. Folks, our first rule of life is: Survival. We need to survive. Everything else is not important or does not matter if we're not here. And survival takes work, it takes being smart, it takes being careful, it takes using good judgment, it takes making good choices and making good decisions, and it takes doing the right things that are often very easy to do and actually pretty obvious. Before I go on with that, let me define invincible for you. Invincible is defined in the dictionary as unconquerable. I define it as one thinking that they are beyond anything happening to them, they are all powerful, that nothing can ever happen to them. After all, these people think, IT IS ME AND NOTHING CAN HAPPEN TO ME! Sorry folks; ain't so. The last time I looked, none of us was immortal or invincible. Yes, it can happen to us. Anything can happen to us. Anything can happen to anyone! None of us, and I stress none of us, myself included, is invincible.

I believe that most young people get hurt or killed as a result of car accidents more than anything else, so I will focus on that part of survival. I think the data and facts would support me on this. To me, there are three cardinal rules for survival as it relates to driving. And they are no surprises to you or me or anyone else, but I'm going to emphasize them again because until everyone abides by them, we are all at risk.

Rule #1: Don't drink and drive. Ever. Never. Never. (Within the context of drinking, I mean drugging also.) I'm not even going to get into the fact that you shouldn't be drinking and/or drugging anyhow. I have my own views on that. I'm proud to say that I don't drink or use drugs; I never have drank or used drugs, so that's how I choose to live my life. Having said that, again, never, ever, ever drink and drive and never, ever get in the car with someone else who is drinking or has been drinking. That, folks, is a given. Your judgment and reflexes are impaired. That's not a risk I'm willing to take. I hope you're not either.

Rule #2: Don't speed. Again, no surprise. You cannot be in total control of your vehicle if you're speeding. And we always want to be in control of our life. Speeding is not cool. In fact not only is it not cool, it's plain stupid! How many times have I seen someone speed by me, and by the time I get up to the red light, they are right there beside me? They sped to wait at the light longer than I did. How much do you gain by speeding? How much time do you really save? Here's the real question: Not what do I have to gain by speeding, but what do I have to lose? That, my friends, can be your life or someone else's life. I'm not willing to take that risk either. I hope you're not also. (Also, regarding speeding: please don't rush to get anywhere. Often when we rush, we do things and make decisions that we might not have otherwise made because we were running late and/or rushing to get some place. That also goes back to using good judgment and being on time; then you don't have to rush.)

Rule #3: Always, always, wear your seat belt. I don't care if you're driving your car out of the driveway to park it on the street or the other way around. Wear your seat belt. Get used to it. Get into that habit. Make it part of your routine. If for any reason there is no seat belt in the car for you, then there are too many people in the car. Get out and either don't go or wait for the next car. Always, always wear your seat belt. It's so easy and it's a no-brainer.

I will add a quick four more rules that may very possibly save your life or the lives of others: 1) Pay attention to what you're doing while driving, and that is focusing on the road at all times. Always keep your eyes on the road. You don't need to look at people when you're talking to them if you're driving, and you shouldn't be playing with any kind of electronics. Keep your eyes fixed on the road. It only takes a split second for something to happen. 2) Don't talk on your cell phone or text while you're driving. 3) Always stop for red lights and stop for stop signs. 4) Don't drive if you're tired. Make sure you are well-rested and fully awake before you get behind the wheel of a car. I believe that if you follow all of those basic, simple, and easy-to-follow seven rules, *you will increase your survival rate by 95%.*

Quite honestly, these are all no-brainers. Most deaths and serious injuries in cars are caused because of people not following these really very simple rules; breaking any one of those rules and/or a combination of them can and may very well lead to people getting hurt, seriously injured, and even killed. One of those people could be you or me, or someone in your family, my family, or someone else's family.

Last year when I had the pleasure, honor, and privilege of speaking at the senior's graduation, I told them and the audience: Life is to enjoy, not to get through. Don't do stupid stuff, and what's your hurry anyhow? I will add this for you: Yes, life is to enjoy, not to get through, but you've got to be here to enjoy it. You've got to survive first and you are not invincible. In order to thrive, you must first survive. I always say: WHEN I WAKE UP IT'S A GOOD DAY...BECAUSE I'M HERE AND NOT SOME PLACE ELSE... I want you to say the same and I want to see all of you this year, next year, the year after that, and yes, even the year after that and so on, cross that stage. I do not want to see one empty seat at graduation. Please heed the call. Enough said.

Endnote to Health and Safety: Safety not only pertains to being cautious and careful regarding driving, it also entails always being aware of your environment, staying away from criminal activity, drugs, guns, and gangs. Any one of those activities, or a combination of any of them, will seriously jeopardize your safety and the safety of others. And the question we always have to ask ourselves is why would we ever put ourselves and/or others in an unsafe and uncompromising situation?

23
The Importance of Sharing

We all have something to share. We have knowledge, skills, stories, experiences, and wisdom to share. It is a shame to keep it to ourselves. This is how we learn. We learn from others through sharing. Teachers do it every day.

There is no greater satisfaction than to teach somebody something you know – to share.

Sharing also involves contributing positively to our community and to our society. We all perform various tasks and responsibilities, either through our jobs or our other activities, which help and support our community. It is important that we all take our responsibilities seriously and share and contribute to the common good.

From a speech to students:
On Sharing and Giving Back

Last night I had the honor and pleasure of attending and speaking at the National Honor Society Induction. I must tell you how proud I and everyone else there was of these fine young people. As I looked at the group, I realized how hard they worked, how responsible they were, and how proud they were of their accomplishments. My main message to them was that they now have additional obligations and responsibilities. I told them that they must now share their knowledge, their skills, and their wisdom. Now they must help others. That is their responsibility now. That is their obligation now. You see, I believe knowledge for knowledge's sake is good. But knowledge to share with others is what really counts. That's what makes our knowledge important. What good is knowledge if we keep it all to ourselves? After all, what do teachers do every day? They have knowledge, skills, experiences, and wisdom. They share that with us every day. And, students, you too have knowledge, you too have skills, you too have experiences, and you too have wisdom. You, too, need to share those things with others.

The key word here is "share." People who don't share, those who are selfish and self-centered, "the world revolves around me mentality," are those who I believe are so wrapped in themselves that they never really or truly enjoy the satisfaction of giving and sharing. Do you know people like that? They believe that "It's all about them or me." I have news for those people: It's not all about you or me. The world does not revolve around any of us, you or me or them. So let's get over that.

Selfishness is a trait that I don't particularly like or respect. What's in it for me doesn't do it for me. We have to have a sense of community, a sense of consciousness. We have to do things that are right and for the right reasons. Have you ever heard the quote, "Some people look to do good things while some people do things to look good"? Let me repeat that: "Some people look to do good things while some people do things to look good." I am a firm believer that we should look to do good things. I believe that we have a responsibility to not only ourselves, but to our family, to our friends, to our school, to our community, to our country, to the world. I believe in my heart that our job, our task, our duty, and our responsibility is to make this school, this community, this country, and this world a better place every day. I believe that with a passion. I believe that I want to leave this world a better place than it was when I got here. I want it better for my own children, their children, and their children's children. I want it better for all children. They deserve that. I want it better for you. You deserve that.

By having a sense of community I mean working together to make things better for everyone. A community shares with each other. It looks at the big picture, looks at things globally and not what is just in one person's best interest but what is right and what is in every-

body's best interest. A community does what is right because it's the right thing to do. A sense of consciousness means, and I think I told you this once before, if our gut tells us it's wrong, it's probably wrong. If our gut tells us something is right, it's probably right. That's our conscience talking to us. Educators, by our profession alone, are a giving people, a helping people. I believe it is every teacher's responsibility to give every student every possible opportunity to succeed and to try and help each student be successful. I believe it is every student's responsibility to work hard and to do their very best so they can be successful. If both teacher and student are on the same page with this philosophy, quite honestly I don't see how anyone cannot be successful. I expect that both teachers and students respect each other and trust each other. I would hope that both teachers and students enjoy learning from each other.

I expect that teachers work in the best interests of the students, and I expect that students give 100% every day and take the opportunities provided for them by teachers. I expect that both teachers and students have the passion to be successful. I expect that we, as a school, not only educate students, we provide support for students, we provide encouragement for students, we provide guidance for students, we provide opportunities for students, and we provide hope for students.

I believe that every classroom should have two signs in it, either written or, at the very least, through a sense of feeling when you come in there: One is, "Welcome." The second one is: "Here Lies Opportunity – Help Given

Here. No Cost But Your Very Best." I believe that all of us here in this building – at this school – have a sense of community right here within these walls. I believe that all of us here have a sense of consciousness, a sense of character, and a sense of integrity.

I believe that we are all in this for each other and that our commitment to students is obvious and apparent. I believe that this is a place where all students are embraced and valued. I believe that we believe that every student in this building can be successful. And I also believe that every student has to believe that he or she can be successful. If you have been successful so far, keep it going. If you haven't been as successful as you'd like, the time to start is now. It's a new year. There's no time like the present to get started. It just takes some effort, some confidence, lots of caring, and an attitude change. It's a new year and a new beginning. Go for it. Everyone should commit to sharing and working for everybody's success.

24
The Importance of
Freedom and Democracy

Never underestimate the importance of freedom and democracy. If you don't think freedom and democracy are important, just ask those many millions of people in the world who don't have it. Many lives have been lost and sacrificed in defense of this concept. Millions have died defending it, and many millions more have been wounded. As Americans, as citizens of this great country, the United States of America, though we still have a lot of work to do to make it even better, we have enjoyed the freedoms that most of the world never had and still does not have. We should never take our freedom and democracy for granted.

Many people flocked to this country because of freedom and democracy – the American dream of freedom and opportunity. They still do. Interestingly enough, I don't see people trying to get out of here. I do see them wanting to get in. There is a reason for that and it is the freedom, democracy, and opportunity for a better life. The American Dream still does exist, and we have to keep working hard to ensure its continuity. Having said all of this, we also have a great responsibility to not only keep this way of life going but also to ensure that all of us, all people here in America, have that same opportunity to enjoy the freedoms and participate in the democracy.

I am dismayed and extremely disappointed at the percentage of people in our country who do not exercise their right to vote. That is a travesty. People all over the world would give almost anything to have the right to vote, and some of us choose not to! I don't get that. Some people say their vote doesn't make a difference. What if everyone said that and no one voted? Some people say that no matter who they vote for the politicians do whatever they want. First of all, then do something about that and second, that's not always the case. I'm not going to say that some politicians are not strictly in it for themselves and for the power and prestige. I hope not but I'm not that naïve to think that it does not happen. If that's the case, then it is our obligation and responsibility as the citizenry to do something about it. Vote those people out. We all have an obligation and responsibility to this country, to freedom and democracy, and to become part of the process, even if that means just voting. Voting is power. If we don't use it, then we shouldn't complain. We need to take advantage of the rights and privileges we have – and the power we have.

Some people have said that you get the government you deserve. I don't know that I agree with that, but I will say that we often get the government we allow.

Freedom and democracy also gives us the freedom of choice within the confines of laws and rules and ethical and moral standards that are often left up to society as a whole. Think of the freedoms we do have – freedom of speech, with the obligation of not yelling fire in a crowded movie theater; freedom of the press, without being libelous and scandalous; freedom of assembly, the right to protest, without being violent and mob-like; freedom of religion, to choose to pray as we wish or not to pray at all if we so desire. These freedoms should never, ever be taken for granted. Without them we would be no better than other places in the world that live under oppression and persecution. And we all know that we are far from perfect, but our forefathers have provided us a great foundation upon which we may build a better life for us and for our future generations. The ability to make our own choices and decisions regarding so many things is unheard of in history and today in many parts of the world.

Again, however, though the Constitution and the law say that we are all equal, we know better. We know that some people have not been, and even today continue not to be, treated equally. We need to change that. We know that some people do not have the same opportunities due to their socio-economic conditions. We have a responsibility to change that. We know that, unfortunately, money, skin color, religion, ethnic background, gender, sexual orientation, and physical disabilities often divide us and segregate us. We need to change that. But here's the key and here's the good part: we have the knowledge, the skills, and the resources to change that. The question is, do we have the desire and the willpower to do it?

Government has a responsibility – but so do we, the citizens. We need to work together. We need to be involved. Why we don't sometimes, I'm still trying to figure that out myself.

From a Speech To Students: On Freedom and Democracy

I feel very fortunate today and I need to consistently remind myself that I should feel fortunate every day. I feel fortunate to be able to stand here and speak with you and do so in a free and open society. I am the first to admit that this is not a perfect society by any stretch of the imagination, and the fact that I can even say that in an open forum is proof itself of how fortunate we are to live in this country. I am very proud to be an American, and I am proud that I can criticize my government when I think it is doing something I don't agree with and not fear repercussions. I feel proud to be able to express my views openly and without hesitation. Having said all of that, here is my advice to you as students: Take your responsibilities as Americans seriously. What I mean by that is that you all have tremendous opportunities in this country to be successful, to get an education, to follow your dreams and passions, and to choose a career that you would like to pursue. But it takes hard work and commitment, it takes determination and perseverance, it takes following through on your responsibilities and obligations, and it takes a desire to keep moving forward despite the challenges and bumpy roads you may face as you move along. Don't give up. Never give up. That's not to say that you may not change your plans or direction. It is to say that you should fully pursue your interests and goals. This is part of what makes this country great. You have that opportunity.

Now there are a couple of other responsibilities I want to talk to you about. One responsibility as a citizen you have is to vote as soon as you are old enough. Not voting, in my mind, is not only wrong, it is giving up one of your most cherished freedoms. Always vote. Never not vote. Responsibility number 2, in my mind, is never let anyone or any group take away our freedoms. What I mean by that is no person or group should ever infringe upon the civil liberties that we enjoy in this nation. We are a nation of laws and we are a nation of basic freedoms. It is my hope that we will always cherish those rights and freedoms and that our children and our children's children and so on will always enjoy these very same rights and freedoms. Responsibility number 3 is to understand how our democracy works and become and always stay an informed citizen. Stand up for freedom and for basic human rights, and always have a sense of conscientiousness and community. Know what's going on in your community, your state, our nation, and the world. Stay tuned and stay informed. And responsibility number 4 is do whatever you can to help and support the less fortunate. I believe that a nation is judged on how it treats its most unfortunate citizens. Work to make things better for everyone. We are a community of people and we depend on each other for help and support. Give back to the community as much as you can.

In conclusion, freedom and democracy is not a given. It exists in this country because many people be-

fore us believed in its values and ideas, worked hard to put it together and maintain it, and many more fought to preserve it. The fact that it still exists is a tribute to those who came before us. Nothing happens by accident. It happens because people worked to make it happen. Now that torch has been passed down to us.

25

The Importance of Enjoying Life Despite Not Having Figured It All Out Yet. . .

L ife is to enjoy, not to get through. Enjoy life every day. Live life to its fullest. Laugh lots. Maintain your sense of humor; you'll always need that. Build your positive relationships – knowing, but not dwelling on the fact that it can end at any time and no one knows when or why. Remember, I'm still trying to figure that one out myself also. Keep it all in perspective, looking forward, with hope and optimism and remembering life's lessons and keeping your eye on the ball (don't take your eye off the ball), following your dreams and achieving your goals. Be aware and be conscious about what's going on around you, and keep focused on the positive. Understand that life is fragile and faint, but do everything you can to live as long as you can and to be as successful and happy as you can and help others and inspire others along your journey. My philosophy is that, "I want to do as much as I can for as long as I can." Always try to act in a safe and responsible manner, and be aware of your surroundings and environment. Just be careful, but enjoy.

And, parents, please don't forget, from Crosby, Stills, Nash, and Young: "Teach your children well."

FROM A SPEECH TO STUDENTS:
MY FINAL THOUGHTS TO YOU

And now, you know we have to end with this: For the very last time as high school students: Remember to always: work hard, never give up, maintain your sense of humor, you'll always need that, use your time wisely, always do your very best, have a good, positive attitude, have confidence in yourself and your abilities, be honest with yourself and others, respect yourself and others, think before you act and think before you react, care about and take care of each other and look out and watch out for each other and be kind and nice to each other, treat everyone you meet respectfully and fairly, take responsibility for your actions, always be in control of your attitude, actions and behaviors, always challenge yourself to the best of your abilities, have fun, smile often, laugh with others, not at others, have love in your heart, have a sense of consciousness and community, always show compassion and empathy, follow your dreams and passions, live with a sense of purpose, keep balance in your life, share your knowledge, skills, and wisdom with others and learn from them as well, never give up hope, stay optimistic, maintain your character, integrity, and self-respect, follow through on your commitments, both in your personal life and in your professional life, develop and maintain strong and positive relationships, be a good, trusting friend, take chances in your life but never take chances with your life or the lives of others, stay healthy, always use good judgment, make good decisions and make good choices. And, let's always be careful out there. And – a few new personal comments here special to all of you. No matter where you're off to or where you go from here on in my hopes and wishes for you are: May you always be safe. May you always be healthy. May you be successful. May you be happy. May your dreams come true. May your life be filled with great joy and fun. May there always be more laughs than tears. May your principles and values always guide you. May you always treat everyone the way you want to be treated. May you always have the courage, strength, and ability to continue to move forward and to meet all new challenges. May you do great things, and may you inspire others to do the same. May you make a positive difference in this world, and may the world be a better place because you are here. May your dreams of today become the realities of tomorrow. And, may the best be yet to come. Finally, as always, and most importantly, because all of us here today, including myself, all do very much care about each and every one of you and love each and every one of you, wherever you go, may you always come back to us, and to your family, and to your friends, safely, not just on Mondays, but every day. Thank you for listening and thank you for allowing me to be a a part of your life. Love to you all. And, of course, keep smiling!

Conclusion

Thank you for staying with me. I hope you enjoyed it and got something out of it. This book is intended to ask questions of myself and others and to have each and every one of us ask questions of ourselves. It is a conversation, a dialogue. What is our role in life? What is our role in this world? What is our true destiny? Why are we really here? Truly, I'm still trying to figure it all out myself. After all, that's why I wrote this.

I've tried to raise some questions here. I believe there are some answers and some answers are better than others. There are, at times, situational constraints. Also, what I've written and suggested are not rules – they are ideas and thoughts, concerns and issues to be raised, considered, and talked about. It may be about how things ought to be. Is it a pipe dream? Maybe. But everything that becomes a reality started with some type of idea, ideal, or vision. I can't figure it out all by myself. I need your help, assistance, guidance, and support. This is a group effort. Like I said before, we are all in this together. As Lincoln said, "United We Stand, Divided We Fall." We should never lose our individuality or our freedoms, and we must work together for the common good. Your life depends on it. My life depends on it. Our children's lives depend on it. My father always said, "We should leave the world a little bit better than it was when we got here." Certainly not worse, hopefully not the same. Definitely better. We need to get started.

This is not really just a self-help book; it's a call for raising awareness and, therefore, is truly more of a "Let's Start Cooperating and Working Together To Make It Better For Everyone" book. I don't expect perfection in human beings, but I do expect people to be fair to each other, genuinely nice and civil to each other, considerate of one another, and caring to each other both inside and outside the home. I am not perfect myself by any stretch; I am still trying to figure it all out myself also. Maybe with your help and support we all can make this world a little bit better each day.

I may have left you with more questions than answers. I told you that might happen in the Introduction. I hope at least I've given you something to think about and I've given you some reasons to look at why people act and behave the way they do. I also hope that you will look at yourself to see why you act and behave like you do. Little changes can make a big difference. Little changes are generally easier to do. Big changes – that's challenging. Not impossible, but challenging. I'm also still trying to figure it all out myself. What changes will you make? What will have to happen to make a positive difference in your life?

Remember to be skeptical of people who tell you that they have all the answers and know it all. Also, be skeptical of people who have agendas and who are self-centered and self-absorbed. Watch the manipulators. You need not be paranoid but you do need to be aware and be skeptical. There are people out there who may not have YOUR best interest at heart. I'd like for that to change. That's much of what this book is about.

As I said in the Introduction, I don't know why there is war, disease, genocide, hate, accidents, natural disasters, suicides, murders, other crimes, prejudice, hunger, abuse, mental disease, physical disabilities, and a host of other tragedies, some major and some more minor. We don't know the cards we're dealt and we certainly don't know why we're dealt those cards. I'm still trying to figure that out as well. I don't quite get it. And yet we have to keep remembering that life is good for the most part and we need to focus on that.

There may be lots of important words and concepts that I may have left out or have neglected. If so, I apologize for that. I did not want to overburden anyone or make this book that overwhelming or cumbersome. I tried my best to keep it simple and readable, which was not easy for me!

There may be lots of repetition and overlap and that's okay. We learn it better when we keep hearing it, seeing it, and reading it. Also nothing is in a vacuum or nothing is so perfect and concrete that there isn't overlap. If we do that, we pigeonhole everything. So it is, what it is. And that works for me and, hopefully, it works for you.

I've read two quotes over the years that have had a profound influence on me. One is from Dr. Gordon Livingston, in one of his books, *Too Soon Old, Too Late Smart*, and it says, "No one gets out of here alive." The second quote, and I'm not sure who coined it, says, "Pain and suffering are inevitable. Being miserable is optional." I believe both quotes. Quote #1 is undoubtedly true. Quote #2 certainly has some truth to it. Now please don't take this the wrong way. Certainly at some point we all die (refer, again, to Quote #1). The goal here, however, in my mind, is to live as long as possible, to do as much as we can for as long as we can, and to die from natural causes at a ripe old age and not to die prematurely due to the foolish actions and misbehaviors of either ourselves or other people. Both pain and suffering are miserable, and I can only hope that no one ever experiences either one or both, or at least does so minimally. However, realistically, this is life, and as much as I hope for the best for everyone, I understand that stuff happens. I still don't know why it happens and that's part of what I'm still trying to figure out. I don't know why or understand why we have to suffer sometimes – and I'm still trying to figure that all out as well. In conclusion, I hope that life treats you all well, and wherever you are now in your life, and regardless of whatever has happened to you in the past, may your future be bright and joyful and may the best be yet to come.

L.C.

Afterword

U nfortunately, life does not always turn out the way we had planned or hoped for. The dreams when we were young don't always materialize for all of us as we get older. Stuff happens. More often than not we make it happen or we at least allow it to happen. Sometimes it is out of our control. To a great extent though, we are in control of our own destiny, again understanding that there are some things we cannot control. Much divides us as human beings because we allow it to – race, religion, ethnic background, gender, wealth, etc. – I understand that but I don't like it nor do I necessarily want to accept it. We need to remember those things that unite us more than divide us, and that is that we are all human beings with the same biology, if not the same skills and abilities, and if we were really smart we would combine those different skills and knowledge and work together, dare I say cooperate and collaborate, for the common good and good of all.

I passionately believe that all human beings have a right to, as Jefferson so eloquently stated, "life, liberty, and the pursuit of happiness," and that no other human being or human beings have a right to deprive any person of that right. And I do believe it is a right, not just a privilege. I also believe that good should always triumph over evil. In the ideal world there would be no evil at all. I very much wish that this was the case, and I guess that is the ultimate goal here – to eliminate all evil.

Am I being too idealistic and unrealistic? Maybe so. Actually, probably so. But I can have hope and optimism also, can't I? I admit, though, I'm still trying to figure it all out myself.

Implicit in all of the chapters, hopefully obvious throughout the book, is the importance of always using good judgment and making good decisions and good choices. Most things that happen in life are as a result of choices – those made by ourselves every day, and those often made by others that impact us. In the end, it is the choices we make that ultimately shape our lives – our choices in our attitude, in what we say and do, in how we act and react, in how we behave, and in how we choose to treat ourselves and others. (I would like to sincerely apologize to anyone over my lifetime who I may have offended or was not nice or kind to in any way.)

I know and well understand that we are an imperfect people in an imperfect world. I don't like it, but I accept it. However, that does not mean that we should not try to make it the best we can for everyone. So here's my question and here's my challenge. For you: Do you accept life as it is or do you continuously work and try to change things for the better? For me: Do I accept life as it is or do I continuously work and try to change things for the better? I like to think that I do the latter. I often get frustrated when I don't see a lot of change and improvement. Nevertheless, I'll keep trying. After all, I'm still trying to figure it all out myself. I think we all are. For something to happen, we've got to do something. Let's all work together to make it happen. To quote Viktor Frankl, "I still have something significant yet to do in the future." All of us do. Are we ready for the challenge? Remember, again, it may make a difference to someone and that someone might just be you or me or someone we know, love, and very much care about.

Please let me add one more thing: With whatever issues, problems, and/or challenges you may have, you're never in it alone. Whatever you have experienced or are currently experiencing or going through, others are there or have been there also. Seek the help, assistance, and support that you need. It is out there. It's about finding the right people to talk to. Please don't be afraid to ask for help and get help. None of us can do it all ourselves.

Thank you, again, for taking time to read this book.

With hope for a great future.
Enjoy the ride.
Larry Cohen

COMMENTS AND CONTACT INFORMATION

I sincerely hope that you will follow up with your own thoughts and comments via e-mail:

larry.h.cohen@gmail.com

Again, this is a work in progress for all of us.

I have also set up a website with insights posted weekly:
http://www.larryhcohen.wordpress.com

To order copies of this book directly from the publisher, please go to
http://www.ravenwater.com

Lawrence Hillel Cohen

The author will donate $1 from every book sold to
Lines of Love.

Lines of Love is a new non-profit foundation directly assisting teens struggling with anxiety or depression find the resources they need.

This foundation was created in the memories of two recent high school graduates, Katrina Tagget and Casey Spence, who lost their battles with depression in 2008 and 2009, respectively.

Lines of Love holds monthly events at local schools and communities to raise awareness about anxiety and depression. If you would like Lines to come to your community to raise awareness and help teens benefit from available resources, please do not hesitate to contact us.

CONTACT INFORMATION:
Email: linesoflove@gmail.com
Website: http://www.linesoflove.org
Please join our group on Facebook.
Mail donations and correspondence to: Lines of Love,
P.O. Box 20424, Baltimore, MD 21284

AND AS ALWAYS, AND MOST IMPORTANTLY, COME BACK TO US SAFELY ON MONDAY – AND EVERY DAY.

LOVE TO YOU ALL AND KEEP SMILING.